My Silent Partner

Published by Insight Marketplace
Duxbury, MA 02332
www.InsightMarketplace.com

To purchase additional copies of this book, please visit
http://www.InsightMarketplace.com
Bulk discounts are available for multiple copies. Contact:
CustomerService@InsightMarketplace.com

Visit www.booksurge.com to order additional copies.

My Silent Partner
A Young Entrepreneur, A Seasoned Businessman; And The Greatest Lesson In Business

John Roland

Insight Marketplace
Duxbury, MA 02332
2007

My Silent Partner

Contents

Introduction   xi

The Story

Part I—Reality Bites   1
Part 2—Gaining Insight   31
Part 3—Another Realm   159

The System™

Vision   179
Unity   183
Business Model   189
Passion   195
Strategy   201
Execution   205
Cash Flow   211

Summary   213
A Note on Raising Capital   215
About the Author   219

To Connie, Cole, Kendall and Taylor, thank you for daily love and support.

Introduction

It all comes down to *leadership*. True leadership. Minute by minute, the world changes. Things thought to be permanent are actually an illusion. Technology advances, new markets surface. And all the while, customers' wants and needs quickly evolve. Global business today marches to an incessant rhythm of change and that change is accelerating...even as you read this. Competition lurks in every corner, attacks quickly and takes no prisoners. We're all trying to differentiate and grab each others customers—worldwide. As a business leader you're a part of a giant vortex in constant motion. Gone are the days when a bright entrepreneur could burst on to the scene with a great idea, hone the business model and reap the rewards for years or decades on end. Those were the days of inefficiency, lack of transparency, lack of speed. Today, your idea and business model have a short harvest window. After that, you need to be in position to evolve once again.

Leading in this environment requires that you provide *context*. A context in which your people can succeed. A business, something dynamic, unique and ever-changing—depending on constant innovation as the antidote to change—requires a system that can direct it, guide it, organize it and develop it, but without stifling it. A system that can endure for the ages despite the eternal change. For the past 20 years I have been searching for such a system, methodology or set of best practices. After reading dozens and dozens of books, and yet another dozen, I still hadn't found such a system. I read many books on strategy, some on vision, quite a few on execution and so on. Each time I learned more and implemented the advice, but my quest came up empty. Finally, after many books, many years of experience and an unfulfilled search, I decided to create my own. I named it aptly—The System™.

When running a business, your people are counting on you to find a way to win. So I chose seven sacrosanct principles to do just that: Vision, Unity, Business Model, Passion, Strategy, Execution and Cash Flow. If coordinated to work in unison, they create the necessary context and form a tightly-integrated, perfect system. One that fosters an inspiring vision, unified constituents, a sound business model, passionate employees, an effective strategy, an ability to execute, and an ability to generate positive cash flow. Passion, the power of motivated and engaged employees, lies at the heart of The System™. For your business to survive and thrive, it must be designed at its very core to innovate. And innovation breeds in an environment of creativity, inspiration, speed, constant learning, experimentation and risk-taking. And the only way to create such an environment...is from cultivating Passion. Passionate people motivated to succeed.

Together these principles combine to drive any company and manage a successful business outcome. All principles are interrelated and each reinforces the others to form an integrated whole more powerful than the sum. All must be functioning properly by themselves and all must interoperate seamlessly. The stronger each principle is and the more symbiotic of each other, the faster the company can move through the changing marketplace to generate shareholder value.

What makes this book different is that The System™ isn't about theory, it's about sound business principles, communicated in a simple manner, that can be implemented immediately. And for even further insight and clarity, I wrote this book by encapsulating this real-life system within a fictional story to bring the concept to life and provide concrete examples. At the end, I cover The System™ in detail with implementation notes. Implementing the concepts in this book can help you to gain a distinct competitive advantage over others in your industry.

Whatever your situation, I truly hope that this book helps you improve your business and profit through the changing times. The key is recognizing that everything in business relies on *people*. Passionate people, rallied around a common cause, can create a formidable force and take any hill. Strong teams, able to disagree, but also able to trust and rely on each other, are a key competitive advantage. Advantages like these require true leadership to surface. It comes from providing a vision for which people can strive, a context in which to operate and an environment filled with passion to enjoy the endeavor.

Sooner or Later...

Caroline had never felt so anxious before. Sooner or later the truth always reveals itself, reality gets exposed, and that day was today. It seemed as though her company was falling apart and she was no longer in control. Today she had to face the venture capitalists who had invested millions in her as CEO of UpMarket Media and her summary of the company's performance would not be palatable.

In the early days, with plenty of money in the bank right after funding, everything was so easy, so right. The only objective was to grow. New employees joined the company every day, product development was ongoing, and there was eagerness and excitement in the air for what was to come. Caroline was quoted frequently in the media and UpMarket was at the forefront of its industry.

Now, cash was running low, product development was behind, sales were even further behind, and in general, commitments were not being met. In the back of her mind, Caroline was deathly afraid that this next board meeting would be her last. More than anything, she wanted one last chance to turn things around.

PART 1
REALITY BITES

Board Discontent

"Caroline, I'd like to jump right into the meeting and get down to it if you don't mind," said Reed Johnson, the lead investor in UpMarket. It was Thursday noon in the company's conference room. "We know that performance is just not where it should be and we're still burning a great deal of cash every month. To be blunt, it seems as though the company is broken." Caroline shuddered to hear those words about the company she had started, her pride and joy. It had become part of her persona, her social life, and the one thing she was most passionate about.

Her heart was in her throat, she knew she was on the witness stand defending herself and she didn't have a great defense. Admitting that she lacked the experience needed to be CEO would be a quick and certain death. So instead, she was more defensive and hopeful. "I know that our revenues haven't climbed at the rate we forecast, and we missed this month's revenue target by 25%, but our new product development is almost complete and once we come out with our auto-optimization release we're expecting a lot more volume from our customers." Reed looked down at his lap, away from her pleading face, clearly having hoped for more than that.

Reed was the General Partner at Omni Ventures. Omni was a venture capital firm with a national reputation for backing many successful companies over the past decade. Reed had seen a lot in his day and prided himself on his ability to size up entrepreneurs, to assess whether or not they had what it took to create the next successful company. He was self-assured and if some people didn't care for him, then so be it. Life he felt, and especially his role as an investor, wasn't a popularity contest. He was paid to grow and protect his investments.

Reed was good at what he did and had been very successful over the years. Somewhat private, always careful in his deliberations, he was usually able to sense the risks that lie beneath the opportunities. When he first met Caroline, he knew she was young, but she had a vision, was very engaging and was considered an expert in the industry. However, now sitting in UpMarket's conference room, 10 miles west of Boston, he feared that the risks had blown up into a full-scale crisis. This small 60-person software company was in trouble. And the young woman in front of him was an unhappy reminder that his usual sound judgment could have failed him.

Reed was Chairman of UpMarket's board of directors. As CEO, Caroline had a board seat, and the remaining member was Mark Tobias from Whitepoint Capital. While Reed's company was the lead investor in UpMarket with $4 million in the first round, Mark had invested $2 million "behind" Reed.

Over the last few years Mark's investments had faltered so he was eager to turnaround any "losers" and liquidate the "winners." Sometimes prematurely. To Mark, UpMarket was turning into a loser and he wanted a change...quickly. He had a number of ideas on how companies should be run and he would frequently impress his opinions on young CEOs. Now, impatient to pick up where Reed stopped, he pressed on. "Caroline, we've been through a few board meetings now and nothing you've done seems to be working. As a matter of fact, things are not only not getting better, they seem to be getting worse. I've heard that your management team is concerned and the customers are uneasy. What's going on?"

Caroline countered, "Mark, we have a lot going on. We're trying to grow revenues at an accelerated rate, come out with new products faster than the competitors, train people quickly and build an infrastructure to support the larger company. And we have that new partnership with Asics Technologies that you wanted me to sign. It's consuming a great deal of our product development resources and I'm not sure the benefits are really worth it." Mark didn't like that comment. He was trying to help both UpMarket and Asics, one of his other investments, with a deal that could have benefits for both, but subconsciously he knew it wasn't working for either company. Still, he needed to defend his original position. "Caroline, just give it time, you'll see."

Attempting to show progress, Caroline spent the next twenty minutes reviewing the company's revenue, customer wins, service initiatives, new product development, marketing events and financial results. Both Reed and Mark seemed to be barely listening. Listening as if they had already selected a new CEO and they should be investing their time in that person rather than placating Caroline. It was obvious that the connection she once shared with them had slipped away.

Caroline stopped. "Look…Reed, Mark…I think I know where things stand. We're in a pretty rough situation and things need to change…immediately. I started this company on a shoe-string two years ago and made it through a lot of tough times. Then, last year you invested $6 million and today I only have $1.9 million of the funds remaining. I know we haven't made the progress that I said we would, but things are going to change. They're going to change right away. I'm looking for you to give me that chance." Reed said, "What do you suggest? What's going to be different this time?" "You'll see," replied Caroline with conviction, but yet without a plan. From the look in her investor's eyes, it was unlikely that she'd get that chance.

A Pressing Undercurrent

After the board meeting Mark walked Reed to his car to talk privately. Mark was agitated. "Reed, I think we need to replace her right now. We've pretty much feared this was going to happen, even before we made our investment, but this deal seems to be tanking right in front of us. She's just too inexperienced to turn it around."

Reed threw his briefcase in the back seat of his car and shut the door. He turned to face Mark, not flinching from his close proximity. "Mark, this is a tricky one. First of all, she personally knows every major customer and they trust her. Secondly, there's a heck of a lot of people in the industry that genuinely like her, not to mention all of the key employees at UpMarket. Now I'm as upset at her performance over the past year as you are, but replacing her isn't a slam dunk."

Mark wasn't deterred. "Reed, nothing's ever easy, but we need to get this company back on track. Hell, we're two-thirds of the board—we could even vote on this thing in the parking lot and get it over with. All we need is the new CEO." Reed knew Mark was being hasty, but couldn't argue with his concern. "Alright, Mark, take a look and see if you can find out who's out there on the market, but keep it quiet. Let's take a little time and do this right. By the way, just for the record, she has more energy, passion and enthusiasm than most of the CEOs in my portfolio companies."

Mark had what he wanted. "Well, that may be so, but if we don't make a move soon, she's going to run out of money. And no new CEO worth their salt is going to come into a company burning cash and with no money in the bank. So we'll be forced to support the company with more capital or end up getting diluted by someone else's investment." Frustrated, Reed opened the door to get into his car. Yet again Mark rushed to the conclusion. "Mark, don't go there yet, just see what you can find out."

The Early Days

Although Caroline Ford was attractive, what made her standout was her fashionable style. It was never over-done and her presence was so subtle that people who met her were never quite sure why she made such a strong impression. With light-brown hair, brown eyes and a runner's physique, her most striking feature was her inviting smile. It lit up her face and grabbed your attention. As a result, all her life people were naturally drawn to her. At 28 years old and the CEO of her own company, she was standing ahead of the pack amongst her peers. On the downside, she didn't have a lot of friends that could relate to her trials and tribulations.

Caroline graduated from Lehigh University as a political science major. After college, she worked for four years at Carat Fusion, a major advertising agency in Boston. Her first role was Assistant Account Executive working on one of the foremost automotive brands. It gave her wide exposure working on creative campaigns that incorporated all of the major media.

Like most new-born AAE's, Caroline's responsibilities were largely administrative and her access to top decision-makers limited. However, her boss was a strong, generous mentor, and Caroline was a quick study, lapping up everything around her. Soon, it became readily apparent to her that the landscape of advertising was changing. At the agency, her co-workers obsessed over traditional media schedules, expensive production budgets, and reaching the ever-elusive 18-34 demographic through network and cable TV. Yet all around her, her generation was busy text messaging, surfing online or playing video games. The demand for online advertising was exploding while the demand for TV, radio and print was flat at best. And, she thought, not many people in the ad agency world were doing much about it.

At the time, few people knew the dynamics of online advertising, but to Caroline, it was pure gold. It seemed obvious to her that the next boom would be distributing advertisers' banner and video ads on publisher's websites like MSN and ESPN and the countless others. She became fixated on it. As more and more of the Account Managers turned to Caroline to coordinate the online advertising aspects of their campaigns, the agency named her to head a newly formed Interactive Division. She quickly became recognized as a young expert and innovator in the rapidly-evolving field.

First-hand, Caroline saw advertisers' demand intensify for the burgeoning medium, but she also felt their pain and frustration working with multiple vendors, competing technical standards and uneven quality. Most of all she knew that advertisers wanted stewardship of their brands and the ability to control where their online ads were viewed. That meant displaying ads only with reputable publishers that had a proven, professional web presence.

Then she put it all together: her sense of where the industry was headed, her passion to create a product that shaped the future, and the fact that she strongly believed the next decade was going to be a period of massive growth leading to a completely new paradigm. So, she thought, what if she could create a software company that guaranteed advertisers' brands would only be displayed on the websites of reputable publishers? Each publisher in her envisioned network would be included only when fully vetted for reputation, a quality website and appropriate traffic volume. All she needed was the resources to turn her idea into reality.

At a summer party thrown by the agency, Caroline was introduced to an ambitious software developer by a friend. Jake Porter had been laid-off by a Boston-area, online advertising startup and was now biding time working as a contractor on piecemeal projects. They spoke for hours. And before the end of the party, she was sure she had found a kindred soul who understood her way of thinking and had the same passion for innovation. That's the moment when it all came together. Caroline was an entrepreneur at heart, a dreamer, and had watched others around her start businesses with varying success. She wanted to be next. So with great ambitions and a $50,000 loan from her supportive mother, she left the agency and founded UpMarket. Her first hire was Jake Porter.

Jake began programming immediately. He was a machine when it came to churning out code and developing the product. Day and night he worked tirelessly. After six months they had a beta version of their product, the beginnings of an ad network, and a few small clients. And then they caught on fire. After just one year, they had several key clients, a burgeoning ad network, and a unique software product that was in demand. And they were being courted daily by the venture capitalists.

Second Time Around

Immediately following the Dot.com crash, investors were skittish about the online advertising companies after witnessing their meteoric rise and fall. Most of the startups had gone out of business and many of the larger players that remained had lost as much as 90% of their market value. But it had been four years since the crash, and by the time Caroline was seeking major funding, the mood had changed. Like so many innovations before—railroads, air travel, and the introduction of PCs—there was always an initial stage of hysteria and investment speculation, and then the inevitable crash. After that, began the long, profitable stage of secondary investment and growth.

When she first met Reed, Caroline had ten employees and had been in business a little over a year. The economy and market had rebounded, and investors could sense that on this go-around, the Internet was for real. Online advertising startups were back and this time they would live up to their promise of fundamentally changing advertising. This was going to be big and once again the venture capital community found itself chasing them. It was amidst this resurgence that

Caroline met Reed, then Mark, and within a few months, had secured $6 million in venture capital.

Attracted by her idea, both Mark and Reed were secretly committed by the time the initial pitch was over. Caroline's greatest strength was engaging and persuading people to her cause; they were no exception. The same skill that enabled her to start UpMarket and raise capital, also helped her attract a high-quality and experienced management team. And she was at her best when in front of customers and with potential employees looking to join the company. Her passion and enthusiasm could make you feel as if you were missing the opportunity of a lifetime if you didn't join her.

Before the funding, her company was growing, on the move, gaining recognition, and investors wanted in. She was at the pinnacle of her short career. But that all changed. One day at a time. She'd never run a venture-funded company before, never had access to so much money, and now, her decisions didn't seem to be panning out.

Amidst the turmoil, Caroline had a great sense of responsibility for UpMarket. Naturally, she took ownership for anything that she committed to and became emotionally bound. It made her dependable, a quality that Reed, among others, had come to appreciate over the past year. However, it was this sense of responsibility that was now eating at her. UpMarket was her offspring. How could they ask her to step aside?

Coming To Grips

Shortly after the board meeting, Caroline left work early and went home to her apartment on Beacon Hill. She was still stunned and needed to get out of the office. She knew her management team wanted to know how the board meeting went, but she chose to avoid their questions until her mind cleared and her attitude was more positive. She'd call them later to give a few scant details and then see them in the morning.

It was a beautiful, sunny day, but a little cool for early July. It always took a while for summer to warm in New England. But it was a perfect day for running and Caroline was an avid runner. She ran competitively for her high school team and maintained her passion through the years. It was late-afternoon by the time she got home and changed. Normally she'd run four miles or so, but today was going to be a long one. She'd just keep running and running until she couldn't run anymore. Perhaps that would release her heavy anxiety.

As Caroline ran she focused straight ahead barely noticing the sidewalk scrolling under her feet. She was running along the Charles River headed for Harvard Square. After a few miles her anxiety slowly morphed into depression. Then anger. It wasn't fair. She had started UpMarket and no one would even be there if it wasn't for her. Now they were trying to push her aside? As she ran she became more and more enraged, running faster and faster and more effortlessly as each mile passed. All at once anger and fear, frustration and depression were coursing through her, but as she ran, determination and resilience slowly began to take their place. By the time she turned around, well past Harvard Square, she had reached a decision. She had never failed at anything this badly before and she wasn't about to start, especially with the one thing that she was most passionate about.

After ten miles of pounding the streets and sidewalk along the river, Caroline wilted back into her apartment. It was on the tenth floor of an old brownstone. It had a common deck overlooking the Charles River by the Esplanade where small sailboats and college crew boats darted endlessly in the water. She checked her Blackberry for messages; there was one from Reed.

"Caroline. Mark and I were discussing our meeting today. We're going to give you another ninety days to show us that you can turn this company around. That's not a lot of time, and I want you to know, we're going to start sending out feelers for a new CEO right away, just in case it doesn't work out. I must admit, my confidence is shaken at this point, but I invested in you initially because I thought you could do the job. I'm going out of town for a few days, but please give me a call Monday so we can discuss."

Was this good news because now she had been given a ninety-day shot to turnaround the company? Or was it purely lipservice and they were days away from bringing in a new CEO? Either way she knew she had very little time. She sat on the couch in her living room still sweating from the run looking blankly across the coffee table and wondering what to do, who could she call. Then it came to her. And the more she thought about it, the more sense it made. A spark of hope returned. Softly she said to herself, "He'd be able to help."

The Connection

Caroline had a lot of friends, but with such limited time, she chose to spend it with those closest to her. Nancy Hamilton was one of those friends. She had been Caroline's UpMarket sounding board for the past few months. While she couldn't provide a lot of help with running the business, Nancy provided the needed emotional support. The next day, Caroline called her at work. After catching up for a few minutes, Caroline steered the conversation toward UpMarket. At first she hesitated before getting to the purpose of her call, but she knew she didn't have a lot of options...or time. "Nancy, you know I've been struggling with UpMarket for a few months now. I could really use some experienced advice and was wondering...do you think your Dad could help me with this?"

Nancy was Caroline's oldest friend. They attended high school and Lehigh together. Nancy's Dad, Tom Hamilton, was in his early 60's and a successful businessman who had started, built and sold several companies over the years. Tom even gladly admitted his few failures, since in hindsight, he didn't view them as failures, but as lessons learned that contributed to his even bigger successes. "Absolutely," Nancy assured her, "You know he loves you!"

Fortunately, Caroline's timing was perfect. Tom's most recent business was a software company that he'd built over a five year period and had just sold. He declared that he had enough of business and wanted to retire. He wanted to spend more time at home with his family and on things he really loved. The only problem was that he really loved business.

It was Friday afternoon when Nancy called her Dad and let him know of Caroline's situation. He immediately wanted to know how he could help. He'd known Caroline since she was a little girl and always thought highly of her. "Nancy, see if Caroline can meet me at the Starbucks here in Weston on the corner of Centre and Willow at ten o'clock tomorrow. We'll see if we can figure out what's going on."

A Safe Harbor

The next morning Caroline drove out to Weston and found the Starbucks. It was a unique location for the coffee chain. It was in a self-standing wood building that looked like an old "General Store" with a farmer's porch. In the middle of the roof facing the street, where the store sign would have been, was the familiar Starbucks green and white mermaid. However, the inside was the typical modern-day coffeehouse format. In the corner by the front window, Tom had secured the two dark-green velvet, oversized chairs that were crouching low to the ground.

As Caroline walked in the door she immediately saw Tom and waved. He was tall with silver hair and a quarter inch, neatly trimmed silver beard. Blue eyes glinted from behind thin, square, gray-rimmed glasses. He had a distinguished presence about him and a certain confidence that was comforting. Caroline was glad to be in his company.

Tom greeted her warmly. "Hello Caroline! It's been a couple of months since I've seen you! How's your family?" She did her best to convey her trademark smile. "Well, things are great with my family, but I've been better professionally," she admitted.

Tom could see the unhappiness in her eyes. "That's what I heard. How about we get a cup of coffee and then you can tell me all about it?" Caroline was comforted to have an experienced sounding board, someone to confide in who could relate to what she was going through. At the counter he ordered two lattes: vanilla for himself and pumpkin-spiced for Caroline. Tom paid for the coffees and waited in the pickup line while Caroline protected their two strategically-located chairs. Tom retrieved the lattes and sat down next to her. "Okay, so tell me what's going on." Caroline didn't know where to start, so she plunged in with the most recent board meeting.

"Well, as you know I started my software company about two years ago. Everything was going just fine for the first year, so much so, that we started getting attention in the media and I had investors calling *me*. I was "lucky enough" to raise $6 million from two East-coast VCs, but that's when things started to change. At first it was great, but fast-forward to today and now I'm more than two-thirds through the capital and nothing's been working. I'm not hitting the revenue targets I forecasted, a new release of my software is delayed, and my sales team is losing confidence because we've been talking about the release for months now and the customers wonder if it's all vapor-ware. And, best of all," she said sarcastically, "the two VCs that invested in my company are ready to throw me out for a new CEO!"

"Wow, that's a lot to carry by yourself." Tom didn't seem shocked. He'd seen his share of fires in his day. "So why do you think things aren't working?" Caroline continued on. "A number of things. First, our pricing isn't right. We seem to be pricing our service too high and I want to lower prices, but I'm afraid that if I'm wrong it'll only hurt revenue even more in the long run."

"And my CTO is being really difficult. He wants to develop the products his way and he's not working well with me or my VP of Marketing who really know the customers. And, one of my VCs has me engaged in partnership with another software company—also in his portfolio—and it's consuming a lot of our resources that should be concentrating on the core products." Caroline went on enumerating everything she could think of that was wrong. All the while Tom just nodded and asked probing questions. Finally Caroline was done, her shoulders relaxed as she slowly melted back into her chair. It was cathartic being able to release the whole story. Especially to someone like Tom who would understand and maybe help her do something about it. She waited for his reaction. Maybe he could dispense enough wisdom so she could start fixing the problems all at once!

Tom was quiet for a moment. He was certain that Caroline was indeed in trouble and the situation might be too far gone to fix, but he wanted to help. Many years ago he and his family had lived across the street from the Ford family. Nick Ford had been a good friend. It was only a few years since the tragic car accident that had taken Nick's life, way too soon. Tom remembered him fondly. Family connections aside, he thought highly of Caroline and could see that she needed his advice. Besides, he felt it would be interesting to "even up the sides" a little.

Finally, he spoke. "Okay Caroline, that's some story. VCs can be tough, but unfortunately that's the name of the game when you bring investors into your company. And I think you can probably take them at their word when they say they're looking for a new CEO, but they'll need a transition period and that's why they're pretending to give you time to turn things around. They know you won't leave in the interim." Caroline cringed. It was hard to hear the brutal truth.

"So here's what I suggest. You need to focus on controlling what you can control. As long as you're CEO today, you can run the company as you see fit. So why not take control and see if you can turn this thing around?" That got her attention. That's what she was looking for. Some measure of hope. "Tom, I was hoping you'd say that, but I have to ask a favor. What are the chances you could help me?" The silence that followed was agonizingly long. She couldn't tell if he was surprised at her question. She didn't want another disappointment at this point, and besides, she really needed his help.

"I'm pretty confident that I wouldn't be able to help you in just one short get-together...like today." Tom told her at last. "You've got a lot going on here. But I am confident that if we met regularly, we might be able to dig deep enough to get to the bottom of all this." Caroline's face brightened. She pulled herself onto the edge of her seat. She wanted to appear alert and ready and show him that he wouldn't be wasting his time working with her. "From what you've told me, it sounds like you're a natural innovator, but there are a few key elements that every business needs to harvest that innovation. These elements provide structure and if you don't have that structure then you can find yourself all over the place, operating randomly, and stomping out one burning fire after another." Caroline chuckled. "I thought my feet felt hot."

Caroline was relieved and excited at Tom's offer, but was momentarily cautious. "Are you sure you want to do this? I mean aren't there more important things that you could be doing? What if I offer to bring you on as a paid consultant or arrange a block of stock options for your time?" Tom smiled. "Thanks, but actually, I'd enjoy this. And no need for any compensation. I've built a number of companies in my day and I'm not so sure that I want to build another one, but I'd sure like to help you with your company. I'll be your mentor... a silent partner."

Caroline was surprised and moved by his generosity. "A silent partner, I don't know what to say?" He smiled. "Just say you'll meet me back here tomorrow for our first real meeting. After that, we should probably start meeting every Saturday, right here if you like." Caroline confirmed. "Let's do it!"

"And here's the first thing I need you to do for tomorrow. Think of why you started your company, what you wanted to achieve, where you wanted to take it." Caroline looked at him a little oddly. She had no time for historical review or philosophical discussions. She was hoping that they would start immediately fixing things. But instead she said, "OK, I can do that. And any chance we can talk about pricing?" Tom gave her his you-don't-get-it-yet-but-you-will smile. "Caroline, I'm no expert on pricing, but I do know there's a lot more going on here. Let's start at the beginning to see what we can find out. If I'm right, I think we'll see that pricing has little to do with your real issues."

Initial Doubt

Caroline stayed in that Saturday night. It was 9:30pm and she was tired and wanted to be alone. Most of her friends were out while she was sulking in her apartment, dealing with her fate as CEO of UpMarket. It was a rainy, gloomy night, perfectly matching her sentiment.

Collapsed on her couch, she thought about Tom and their meeting this morning. She was excited to have him on her side, but why was he asking why she started the business and where she wanted to go with it? After all, she had real issues to deal with including an obstinate CTO, a sales team that wouldn't sell, and VCs all over her back.

Caroline knew Tom was successful, and that he had built several software companies before, but he had made all of his money in the eighties and nineties and times were different then. Her world today was the domain of the fast-moving, ever-changing Internet startup. Everyday a new company surfaced somewhere in the world with a new way of doing things. Innovation was rampant. Companies that made it went from zero to the moon in a matter of a couple of years. She wondered if Tom knew the new paradigm and what made these companies successful. She couldn't afford to waste any time. Everyday was precious.

Still, she reminded herself, this was Tom Hamilton. He was more successful than anyone she knew. He had to know what he was doing. She decided to give him the benefit of the doubt. Besides, what other choices did she have? Before preparing her answers for Tom, she decided to clean up a few emails. That would allow her to think freely without worrying about what unpleasant news might be lurking. What Caroline wanted was to make it through her inbox without a fire...for just one night.

Her first email was from Deepak Casner. Deepak, in his mid-thirties, was her VP of Marketing, but she also considered him a real friend. He joined UpMarket at the very beginning leaving Microsoft's marketing machine to join her little startup when there were only five employees. Deepak was short and round and could always tell when Caroline needed to talk. Like Caroline, he was a very effective communicator. His email read, "Caroline, please let me know if you're OK with the new brochures and collateral packages. I'd like to print 10,000 kits on the first run and do it ASAP. Sales is all over me to get this done. Thanks! Deepak." Caroline certainly wasn't in a mood to be spending money. The cost of ten thousand kits would be steep. She was conserving cash now, not spending it. "Deepak, we're going to have to delay printing the kits. I'll explain on Monday. Enjoy your weekend. Caroline."

An email from Andrea Johnson, UpMarket's CFO was next in the queue. "Caroline, I just closed the books for June and you know how we thought we'd miss our revenue numbers by 25%? Well, unfortunately it was 30%. We had to issue a credit for Taylor Advertising and it just came out of the blue. Sorry to be the bearer of bad news. Please give me a call when you get a minute. Andrea."

Andrea was 38 years old and had been with the company for just six months. However, Caroline already knew that she was a great find. Andrea was focused on driving results every day, likely a hold-over from her days as an All-American volleyball player in college. As you'd expect from a CFO, Andrea was analytical and detailed, but she was surprisingly supportive of spending money where it needed to be spent to grow the company. At least that was true before they started missing their revenue targets. Caroline decided not to let the email get to her. She figured that things were bad enough and piling this extra bit of bad news wasn't going to change the overall situation. She'd communicate it to Reed and Mark on Monday.

After another email from Deepak, an email from John Chen, her CTO, was next. Without even reading it, she felt her chest tighten. She'd struggled so much with John over the past few months and they just weren't getting along. John joined UpMarket right after Reed and Mark made their investment. He was "recommended" by Mark Tobias who felt that Jake Porter, her star developer, wasn't up to the task of being CTO.

John Chen was in his early forties and she always wondered if, for starters, he resented that his boss was so many years his junior. His email read, "Caroline, unfortunately we're not going to make our latest release deadline again. My guys are all working as hard as they can, but Marketing simply asked us to do too much. Please give me a ring. John."

Caroline's first reaction was anger. Were the software developers truly working as hard as they could? Were they working as hard as everyone else? Did they know how important the auto-optimization release was to UpMarket? It was a big innovation that they had in development for the past six months. The new release would give advertisers an automated process to test different creative messages and determine which ones garnered the biggest response. This release would replace the tedious task of optimizing manually and was heavily anticipated. Clearly it would increase their advertisers ROI as well as boost UpMarket's revenues. And it was only a matter of time before their competitors introduced an equivalent product. What was taking John's team so long?

Or, was the problem that John was diverting some resources to his own innovation project? His idea was to repurpose some of the existing UpMarket code into licensable software, so that large publishers with their own sales teams could purchase and manage their own online ad inventory. It would create another revenue stream from the similar base of software. John's innovation was appealing, but off the mark in terms of UpMarket's core business.

John was very competitive which made him a great asset...when he was on your team. He liked the world to be predictable, ordered and planned. He was instantly on guard against the marketing department which was always making changes. He liked even less the constantly evolving demands of customers. Some thought he was a control freak, but Caroline acknowledged that his coding and engineering practices were tight and his products were dependable with very few bugs. But overall he was perceived as inflexible, a bad fit in a rapidly-evolving industry.

Now Caroline emailed back, "John, obviously this isn't good. Please see what you can do over the weekend to catch up and hit the release date. It'll impact sales, marketing, finance—everything—so I want to think about our options over the weekend. Let's discuss Monday morning. Caroline."

The next email was spam. "Do you want to be a match-maker? Come join the ranks of Internet Singles and connect with the legions making great money by helping singles get together and find their perfect loved one!" Caroline deleted it and smirked before moving on. At least she had a backup career if things didn't work out at UpMarket.

"Pepsi Restless!" This was the subject line of the next email from Keith Cavanaugh, UpMarket's VP Sales. "Caroline, we didn't have a great meeting with Pepsi today. They're getting restless and I'm concerned that they're pulling away from the budget they originally gave us. This means 20% of next year's revenue's in jeopardy. And I heard that they were calling in Xenic for a presentation. Let's talk. Keith."

Caroline's heart sank. Pepsi was their largest customer. Xenic Systems was their arch-nemesis. Why couldn't the bad news stop for just one day? She checked her IM and saw that Keith was still online. "Keith, it's Saturday night, no life either?" Keith got the humor and responded immediately. "A life of little kids and no baby sitter! Did you get my email?" "I did. How about you get everyone that touches the account together Monday morning. We'll throw everything we've got at this if we have to." Keith was cheered by her tenacity. "Sounds good Caroline. Get some rest. We'll tackle this Monday when we're all a little fresher and can think more clearly."

For her part, Caroline appreciated Keith's upbeat manner. He was a consummate salesman. Always well-dressed and very articulate, and as you'd expect, he enjoyed winning others over...especially new clients. He was good at maintaining existing relationships too, but if he had a preference he'd leave that to customer service and spend more time deer hunting. Keith was a good guy she thought, but somewhat political and would rarely show his cards either way when it came to controversy. He came into UpMarket via a recommendation from Reed Johnson. Previously, Keith had worked at one of Reed's portfolio companies and did a great job. Caroline knew that Reed respected Keith and that they talked now and then. Although, Caroline always wondered how much they talked about her and UpMarket.

Scrolling through more emails, she hurried through one from their new partner Asics Technologies asking if UpMarket was going to share a booth at an upcoming trade show. After that she received an email from Beth Jarvis, her VP of Customer Support. "Caroline, I just heard from Keith about Pepsi. I think I know what's going on and what caused the problem. Please give me a ring when you get a chance. Beth" Beth was 27, and one of Caroline's hardest workers and biggest supporters. And she was very loyal to the company.

However, execution wasn't her strong point, perhaps because of her relative inexperience in management, and now and again, it caused problems with clients. She sent Beth a quick reply, "Beth, Keith is going to organize a meeting for Monday morning and we'll determine what needs to be done then. Please make sure you can make it. Caroline."

When Caroline reached the end of her email inbox she sat back and reflected. Each day was taking a lot out of her emotionally. It hadn't been like that in the early days, before the new investors came on board. She decided to get a good night's sleep and start working in the morning. Before dropping off into sleep, she remembered that good feeling she had had with Tom Hamilton, and the hope that he could provide some answers. That made her sit straight up and remember his questions for her. So she propped up her pillow, sat back and thought, "Why *did* I start this company? Why are we all here? And most importantly, where are we going?"

PART 2
GAINING INSIGHT

A Journey Worth Taking

It was Sunday morning and Caroline walked up the farmer's porch steps of Starbucks to meet Tom. She felt the warm sun on her face. She wished it could be just any Sunday morning. She'd go for a run, enjoy the weather by the Charles and relax for the day. Instead, she was trapped in a difficult situation, searching for a way out.

Inside Starbucks, she noticed Tom in the now-familiar corner. Remembering Caroline's order, he had two lattes waiting for them on the small round table and was reading through some papers. Caroline sank into the open chair. "Good morning and thanks for the latte! Still sure you want to do this?" He smiled. "Absolutely. Actually I'm looking forward to it." Caroline asked, "What are you reading?" Tom straightened the papers on his lap to align them. "Just some information off your website. I wanted to see if I could get a little better understanding of your business before we began." It comforted Caroline to know that he was taking this seriously.

"Okay Caroline, I want to go over why you started your company and where you want to go with it. Does that make sense?" Caroline wasn't sure. "Well, kind of, but why not start with the most pressing issues?" Tom knew he had to backup a little and explain. "You see, before we can work on some of your more difficult issues, we need to understand UpMarket's purpose and vision. Your purpose describes why your company exists and gives everyone's daily effort meaning. By holding it high, your employees can connect with the company and rally behind it. And your vision builds on that and inspires your employees to reach some greater destination or rally behind some passionate cause. These are important things to get right because every other decision at your company needs to fall inline with them. So before we can start the triage on your problems, we need to know why we're here in the first place and where you're going. Make sense?" Caroline nodded. "Okay, so let's start with your purpose. Have you given any thought as to why you're in business?"

"I have," said Caroline. "Let me see if I can explain. I started my business because I saw an opportunity to improve the way online advertising was managed. Our software and the network we've built provides a higher quality venue for our advertisers to run their online ads. That, in turn, increases the response rates and overall ROI of their online campaigns. We're pioneers leading the way in a rapidly changing industry." She knew that didn't sound very compelling.

Tom thought for a moment and said unconvincingly, "Okay, that's good, that's good, but I think we can do better. What you just described addresses the benefits of your product to your customers more than anything. Remember what a purpose is. It's about achieving clarity on the reason why your company exists, finding its true meaning."

Caroline thought about it. "Okay, well if that's the definition, then I think the reason why we exist is to lead the evolution of online advertising. I've always had a pretty good idea of where the industry needs to go." Tom slowly nodded to draw more out of her. "Good. Now we're getting somewhere." Caroline added a follow-up thought. "With innovation. Relentless innovation. That's our purpose." Then she pieced it together. "To lead the evolution of online advertising with relentless innovation." Tom pulled back in surprise. "Wow! That's good. Now that's a purpose that employees can understand and want to be a part of. Nice job." Caroline absorbed the compliment. It felt good to be praised again since she hadn't heard those words in a while.

Tom continued. "Now, let's build on that. What we need is to articulate your vision for UpMarket. All truly great companies have an inspiring vision. Why? Because the most important thing you can do when running a business is provide leadership. And if you're leading people, they expect to be led somewhere. So the key question is, now that we know your purpose and *why* your company is in business, what we need now is to know *where* you're leading everyone. Your investors, your board and employees."

Caroline sat back and let his comments sink in for a minute. It made sense to her, a lot of sense. "I never thought about it that way Tom. I always felt I had a vision for UpMarket, but now I see that I wasn't fully using it. More than just something to engage customers and investors, it can be used as a tool to lead people."

"That's right. When everyone in your company is inspired by some great vision, they think more creatively, ideas flow more easily and they have a can-do attitude. It compels employees to do something great and be a part of something bigger than themselves. It creates focus for everyone in the company. It generates enthusiasm and dedication and lets the employees know that their work really matters." Caroline could see the passion in Tom's eyes.

"Answers to the questions 'Why do we exist?' and 'Where are we going?' should be simple for a business leader to answer right? You'd be surprised at how many companies don't have a stated purpose and vision. You can't do anything else properly until you've figured it out. For example, you can't effectively plan a strategy. To achieve what? Go where? You can't properly hire people. What skills do they need? Those companies need direction. And, the most short-sighted thing you can do is create a company simply to make money. Those have the hardest time existing because there's no 'there' there."

"And at some other companies, the only vision is to sell to Google, Yahoo or Microsoft in three years. That's not a vision, that's a financial exit. A vision is separate from any financial, strategic or operational goal. When you know your vision and how you want to impact the world, you set your company apart. That's what attracts people. That's what motivates them. That's powerful!"

Tom leaned forward. "Okay Caroline, you mentioned that you've always had a vision for UpMarket and you've used it to engage your customers and investors. Can you tell me what it is?" Caroline began describing it out loud. "Well, it's obvious to me that within a decade most of the content on network TV, broadcast television and cable will migrate over to the Internet. Same with radio, outdoor advertising and a big part of print. Sure, those companies will still create their shows, news, sports, weather, whatever, but it's all going to be distributed and viewed via the Internet. For example, you'll still see someone like Katie Couric on NBC News, but it won't be shown through existing broadcast channels, it'll come via NBC.com. And, UpMarket will be the company that serves up the advertising around that content."

Tom was getting excited. "Now we're getting somewhere. Keep going. So what would you say is the vision of your company?" Caroline nudged up an inch on her chair. "To revolutionize advertising through transparent marketing." Tom took off his glasses before responding. She was throwing industry jargon at him. "What's that?" Caroline stated it again, but this time added a little more explanation.

"Today, when an advertiser runs an ad on broadcast TV, it's advertising to a particular demographic; let's say 600,000 people aged 18-34 in the Boston area. They're reaching some of those people with their message, but they don't know how many people saw the ad or if they took any action on it. Contrast that with UpMarket's value proposition. Our advertisers pay when a user, viewing content on a publisher's website in our ad network, clicks on their ad. That means for every dollar advertisers spend, they know exactly how many clicks, and therefore how much interest, and potential sales, they generated. The entire process is very transparent and that's why I called it 'transparent marketing.' So my vision is to create the online advertising leader that revolutionizes advertising through transparent marketing. It's the ultimate in efficiency."

It still wasn't working for Tom. "It's okay, but I just can't picture it. To be really powerful, it should bring an image into the person's mind the first time they hear it, even if they're not from the industry. When you can accomplish that, then you know you've nailed it." Caroline offered, "What about... be the leader in online advertising." "Too generic, a lot of companies say that they want to lead this industry or that industry. It's not very inspiring."

Caroline wouldn't let go. She wanted to get it right. "Tom, let me brainstorm out loud for a minute. I know I want to be the leader in online advertising.... to control the majority of advertisements in online advertising as all media migrates online...I want to perform, provide, conduct...coordinate...." Tom prodded her along. "It's coming Caroline, keep working on it." He knew how hard it was to find those exact words to perfectly express the vision.

"In the future," she tried again, "the vast majority of all media will be online and our vision is to be the...to be the software infrastructure coordinating it all. Yuck!" "Caroline, I know it's difficult, but try to keep it clear and concise." She knew she was pressing too hard and it was stifling her creativity. From her agency days, she knew that sometimes the best ideas just popped unexpectedly into your head when you weren't trying. "In the future, the vast majority of media will be online and we provide the software infrastructure coordinating advertising? Wait a minute. I also want to make sure that it states that we control a significant percentage of the market. Kind of like we're in the hub of it all." Tom could sense it developing. "We're close and getting closer." Then it came to her. "To provide the software hub, at the center of all online advertising, coordinating the majority of advertising transactions worldwide."

"Caroline, not bad, not bad at all. Hell, you're even starting to get me excited." Caroline smiled at his approval. "Okay, so here's what you have to do. You have to meet with your management team, your employees, your board and even your customers—all over time—and spread the vision. Get their buy-in, get their feedback. I'd expect that you'll tweak the vision even more based on the feedback which is perfect. It not only makes it more robust, it'll achieve more buy-in."

"Keep in mind that for your vision to be realized it depends on a few other business elements to be in place." That piqued Caroline's curiosity. "What other elements?" Tom held her off. "Hold that thought, we're going to take them one at a time since each one builds on the next. That's why it's important that we get your vision crystallized. Believe me, you don't want to be competing against those companies tightly organized around an inspiring vision. Those companies do things that'll amaze you. They'll land the customer even with inferior products and services because they're so passionate. They'll develop the new product faster and beat you to market because they have something other than just a paycheck motivating them to succeed."

As they were collecting their belongings to leave, Tom looked at her and said, "Caroline, we started our conversation about vision with the understanding that running a business is all about leadership. But know this. It also takes character and emotional fortitude. I know you have it. As a matter of fact I'm quite impressed by how you're handling this. And every great leader only becomes great because he or she had to deal with difficult people and adversity. So expect to continue to be hit with issues from all sides. Handle them one-by-one and keep your decisions inline with your vision." Caroline appreciated the advice. "Okay Tom, thanks for that and I'll let you know how it goes." Caroline was about to see just how many issues there could be.

On The Inside

"Goooood Monday morning from all of us here at WCXT. This is the morning crew and…" Keith powered down his car radio. He was already frustrated with the rush hour traffic and didn't need more agitation from the "zoo crew." Just then he felt his Blackberry buzz so he flipped it out of his holster. "Hey Reed, how's it going?" Reed and Keith only spoke every couple of months, but they had no problem picking up right where they left off. "Keith, do you have a couple of minutes?" Staring at the parking lot of cars in front of him Keith replied, "I've got plenty of time. What's up?"

Reed worked his way into the reason for his call. "I'm taking a couple of weeks off for vacation and before I leave I'm checking in with all of my portfolio companies. I'm particularly concerned about UpMarket so I had a couple of questions if you don't mind." Keith said the only thing he could say. "No problem Reed, what'd you need to know?" Reed began fishing. "How are things progressing at the company? I know sales are falling short, but I don't get the impression that it's a sales issue. I think there're some other things going on." Reed was trying to leave the hole wide enough so that Keith could drive whatever he wanted through it.

But Keith didn't bite. "You know Reed, we're struggling on a few fronts. I know my sales team is a little tentative due to the delayed releases. They should be coming out faster than they are. And I think we could improve our customer service. But overall I think it's a combination of things contributing to our problems." Keith cringed when he heard his own words come out. He knew his answer was vague, but he didn't feel like contributing to a major conflict between Reed and Caroline. Not satisfied, Reed pressed with a direct question. "How is Caroline doing? I know she's young, but do you think she can handle this?" Reed was hoping for some insight. "Good question Reed. I like Caroline a lot, but the jury is out as to whether she has the seasoning it's going to take to get us through this. I will say this, though. She is great in front of the customers and even better in front of the employees. They all trust her, respect her and genuinely like her." Keith was walking a careful line between honesty—he knew Reed trusted him—and his sincere desire to protect Caroline.

They talked for another few minutes, mostly Reed asking questions, and Keith becoming increasingly uncomfortable and evasive. Reed knew Keith was hedging his bets and he didn't want to be overly suspicious so he ended the investigation. "Keith, I've gotta run, but as usual it was good to talk to you. Go attack those revenues and I'll catch up with you later." With that, Keith hung up his Blackberry and stared straight ahead into the bumper of the car in front of him. He thought to himself…they're going to railroad her.

An Unsettled Team

Caroline was energized by her meeting with Tom, but that was soon overtaken by her dread of returning to work and the current host of issues. Her board was looking for a new CEO, the management team was rumbling, and just about every aspect of the company needed her attention. But with a little guidance from Tom, she was more confident, kind of confident, sort of confident, that she'd be able to fix things. It was Monday morning. First she needed to visit a customer about an hour away in Pawtucket to put out a fire, but as soon as that was over she'd be back in the office to get her team together. She had a few things she wanted to discuss.

As soon as Keith arrived at work he zipped past his own office and marched into Andrea's still wearing his golf pullover and his laptop case slung over his shoulder. Like Keith, Andrea had worked at venture-backed companies before and knew the rules. Keith and Andrea weren't exactly close, but they had this mutual connection between them. Relative to the other, younger players, they were the senior, battle-worn executives on the team. "Andrea, I get the feeling that the board meeting didn't go so well and that Reed and

Mark are looking to replace Caroline." Andrea looked up at Keith a little surprised and said sarcastically, "Good morning to you too, Keith. How was *your* weekend?"

Keith grunted. "Andrea, I mean it. Reed just called me, fishing around wanting to know how Caroline was doing running the company." Andrea said, "Well, what did you tell him?" "I was caught a little off-guard, so I didn't quite know what to say. I've known Reed for a long time now and I'm not going to lie to him and at the same time I'm not looking to be the one that gets Caroline booted out of her own company. So I told him that things could be better, and we all have a part in that, but that Caroline was really good at keeping the customers and employees engaged." Andrea frowned. "Not exactly a glowing endorsement Keith." Her lack of sympathy made him defensive. "Well, what'd you expect? We're not exactly blowing the lid off the can now are we?"

Just then John walked by. Stopping to poke his head in, he repeated too loudly, "What do you mean 'with her in charge we're not blowing the lid off the can?'" Keith motioned to John to lower his voice, but his comment was overheard by both Deepak and Beth in their neighboring offices. Within thirty seconds they were in a full swing management meeting with half of them in the hallway, sans Caroline.

Andrea motioned everyone into her office and closed the door. "Listen everyone, as we all know, things aren't going that well. Keith thinks that Reed and Mark are trying to bring in a new CEO." Keith added. "Not only did I get that feeling from my conversation with Reed this morning, but I've seem him do it before, at my last company. As soon as the CEO stops performing, they're out the door. Reed can be fair and cut you a break or two, but if you continually don't perform then he never hesitates to pull the trigger." Deepak spoke up on Caroline's behalf. "Keith, what were you doing talking to Reed this morning anyway?" Keith snapped back. "Listen, I didn't call him, he called me. Besides, I've known Reed for years now."

In the short silence that followed, John pressed his agenda. "I agree, I think that we've been floundering and we probably do need a stronger CEO. I mean you either move forwards or you move backwards and we've been moving backwards for months now." Deepak jumped to the rescue again. "I don't agree. We're all here because of Caroline. She's the one that founded UpMarket and got us to this point. We owe her a lot." Beth agreed. "We need to stay together as a team and work our way out of this mess." Beth was always the consensus-builder. She didn't care for politics and just wanted the management team to get along. Unfortunately, Keith's next condescending comment only added to the tension. "I hate to break the news to you guys, but either you perform in VC-land or you're out."

Andrea didn't want an argument in her office so she diverted everyone's attention with another point. "Listen, there's another person we're not even talking about. Reed is one issue and he's certainly holding most of the cards, but Mark is another. I have friends who've worked at companies where he was an investor and the reviews weren't good. They all say that he can be a one-man wrecking crew. The fact is, Caroline is lacking a little business experience, but she has passion and the relationships with all of the customers and employees. That's what keeps us going." Everyone but John nodded as she continued. "My real concern is that I don't know how she's going to be able to stand up to those two."

Humble Beginnings

That afternoon Caroline was on her way to the conference room for her meeting with the management team. As she walked past the Call Center where the customer service representatives were stationed, she heard the low murmur of voices talking to customers as the Reps sprayed their fingers over their keyboards and glared at the illuminated screens to answer the incoming questions. One of UpMarket's newest employees was sitting in a cube facing the hallway. Caroline approached him and tapped him on the shoulder.

"Hey Sam, how's it going? Are you getting to know your way around here a little better?" Sam rolled his chair away from the cube and swiveled his seat to face Caroline. He was quite surprised. He'd only met her once before on his first day and he was impressed that she remembered his name. "Great Caroline, it's pretty interesting stuff that we're working on and I'm glad to be on board." Caroline fed off the novice enthusiasm. "That's great. Listen, if you have any ideas to improve the Call Center, please make sure that you tell Beth or even email me. Okay? I know you're new here, but that's all the better. You'll have a fresher perspective."

At first Sam didn't know what to say, he had never heard a request like that directly from a CEO. But he knew that Caroline meant it and it made him feel like part of the team. "Will do Caroline. You know, I've got a few ideas already." Caroline smiled her approval and turned towards the conference room. "Sounds good Sam, I look forward to hearing about them."

The conference room had a wide rectangular floor plan with windows all along the far, wide edge across from the door. To the left was the rectangular table where everyone was seated. It was modest, light-brown laminated wood with a conference phone wired through the center. At one end perched a projector trained onto the large whiteboard about ten feet away. As she walked to her left to take the seat at the end of the table, Caroline noticed all eyes were on her. Everyone was anxious to know how the board meeting had gone.

"Okay everyone, this is the first time that we've all been together since the board meeting so I'd like to spend a little time getting everyone up to speed. But before we do that, first I'd like to find out what we're doing with Pepsi."

Keith was ready to report. "Actually Caroline, as you asked, I got everyone together and we've already met for a couple of hours this morning. We have an action plan that I'd like to run by you. We're going to have to present it onsite, in-person, but if we can live up to these commitments and hit the timelines we've outlined, I think we'll have a chance at saving this account." Caroline was happy to have some good news to start the meeting. "Keith, nice work. I'm looking forward to seeing what you wrote up. And I just want the chance to get in front of them. We worked too hard to get this account, we're not going to let it get away from us."

Caroline switched back to the subject everyone was eagerly awaiting. "Okay, now for the board meeting. I've spoken with a couple of you a little bit about it, but now it's time to give the full group an unvarnished summary." She paused and collected her thoughts. "Overall, it didn't go very well. Reed and Mark felt our performance was unacceptable and, quite frankly, I have to agree. I could spend a lot of time drilling into the individual problems we're having in specific departments, but the real issue is that we're not meeting our revenue targets and we're burning a lot more cash than we originally anticipated. As a result, I know they're questioning my leadership."

Instantly, tension filled the room. Everyone knew they weren't performing well, but now that Caroline was openly admitting it, there was an increased level of awareness and exposure. Any last vestige of avoiding reality was eradicated. The investors had confirmed it. And the fact that Caroline came out and told them what Reed and Mark thought of her performance both surprised and impressed them. It takes a lot to make a statement like that in front of your staff. Her comments created an uncomfortable silence. It's hard to follow up a comment like that with something that doesn't sound patronizing.

Deepak broke the silence first. "I think it's obvious that we all played a role in missing our targets. Don't put this all on yourself Caroline." Caroline appreciated Deepak's consolation, but she knew that some of the others didn't necessarily feel that way so she only nodded to him thankfully. She didn't want to openly acknowledge the comment. Keith followed up with a more direct question. "Do you have any idea of what's going to happen? What Reed and Mark are thinking?" Caroline used that query to regain control of the meeting. "Well, they want what's best for the company and so do I. So do you. That's why I'd like to have a little different meeting this morning. Rather than drilling right into the problems, I'd like all of us to take a step back and pull out of the daily grind. We need to review what's going on from a higher vantage point and see if we're making the best choices for UpMarket."

Caroline had their attention. "Let me ask a general question. Does anybody know why we're all here? I mean everyone in the company, what we're trying to accomplish, and just as importantly, where we're going with this company?" It took a brief pause for everyone to digest the question. Keith chimed in first. "Well, until recently, I thought we were all here to get this company through to an IPO. But every day a new challenge arises and seems to make it more and more unlikely." Deepak hadn't forgotten Keith's comment in Andrea's office and had no problem countering him. "I wouldn't phrase it that way Keith. I think we're all here to serve the customer. Don't you agree Beth?" Though he was referring to the basic principle of providing quality customer service, not the recent problem with their Pepsi client, Beth wasn't quite sure how to take it. In a small voice she said, "Well, I guess so."

John sensed it was the right moment to barge into the conversation. "We're all here to build this company and generate a return for the shareholders and ourselves. And I'm not so sure that meetings like this one are helping the matter while there are real issues, like our next release, that we need to deal with." He looked right at Caroline, but she didn't flinch. Caroline was going to take that challenge head on, but she could see that her management team wasn't expecting a meeting like this. They were expecting to dive into the problems of the day, not talk about their purpose and vision. And, customers were calling, the release was slipping, and their direct reports and staff wanted to know what to do next. Why were they taking time for this when there were real fires burning that needed to be addressed?

Before Caroline could respond, Andrea spoke up. "John, I think we're all here to build a great company, something we can be proud of and remember." Caroline bit her tongue and didn't address John for the moment. Andrea was getting closer. "That's right Andrea. Let me explain where I'm going with my question. It seems as though we've lost our way here and that's my fault. But I'm determined to get the situation righted as long as you're all with me." Caroline could feel the tension from John, even without looking at him. "And before we can do that, we all need to know why we're here and where we're going. Identifying our purpose and vision. If we know those two things, then a lot of the answers to our problems will start to surface. And, as the founder of this company, I'd like to give you my thoughts. I haven't done enough of this lately because, like all of you, I've been more focused on the day-to-day problems. But that's going to change.

Caroline thought for a minute how she wanted to phrase it to her team. "Okay, here it is. You all know that I founded this company because I saw a way to have a huge impact on the online advertising industry. Quite frankly, with the way advertising is evolving and everything's migrating online, I believe we can impact *all* of advertising. With our software and the network we've built, we can do a few things that no other company can do." As she spoke, she rose and crossed the room to the whiteboard, to write the newly crafted purpose statement in large script. "And I believe that our true purpose is…'to lead the evolution of online advertising with relentless innovation.' We have some of the brightest people in the industry working for us and we have a real chance to impact the world and set the standards."

Caroline turned and saw that she was starting to get their attention. Everyone had been talking about problems for so long that they hadn't spent much time on the possibilities of the company. It was quite energizing actually. As usual, Keith commented first. "I've never heard you say it quite like that Caroline. I can use that in my sales presentations." Caroline smiled and then laughed. She was caught off-guard by the quick acceptance. Andrea voiced her agreement. "Caroline, I feel the same way. We do have a real opportunity here to impact advertising."

Caroline seized on the momentum. "Thanks, Andrea. Now if our purpose is to lead the evolution of online advertising with relentless innovation, then it's my vision…

everyone ready?…that we can provide the software hub, at the center of all online advertising, coordinating the majority of advertising transactions worldwide." She turned back to the board and wrote this below the purpose statement. From behind her, Caroline heard Beth's voice. "Software hub?" Caroline acknowledged her with a smile. This was all new to them. "Software hub. Like the hub and spoke of a wheel, our software is at the center of all online advertising. That's pretty powerful."

Deepak was following intently. "Let me suggest this…" He had scribbled Caroline's vision statement in front of him and wanted to clarify it a little. "How about we adjust 'advertising transactions' to 'advertisements.' 'Advertising transactions' sounds a little mechanical without an everyday meaning." "Good idea," said Keith. Beth thought it could be better. "It's still missing something, don't you think?" She jumped to the whiteboard and took the marker from Caroline. The team was fully animated; only John was still silent, resisting the progress and enthusiasm.

They talked for quite a while about their vision, adding, subtracting and arguing about the nuances of every word. Then Caroline made a key adjustment. "Let's change it from 'online media' to 'all digital and interactive media.' It's a much bigger play and reflects our belief that all media are migrating online."

Within an hour, a new vision statement had formed on the whiteboard. Caroline read it aloud. "To provide the software hub, at the center of all digital and interactive media, coordinating the majority of advertisements worldwide." Everyone sat back to let it sink in. The silence signaled that they were pleased. The process had created a new sense of connection among the team. Caroline sensed that they all felt like they had a collective vision of which they could be proud, all that is, but John.

Caroline knew it was a great first meeting, better than she had hoped. What had started out a little shaky had turned into something very positive, but she wasn't done. "Now before we start dealing with the issues at hand, let's all agree on one thing. After this meeting, we're going to spread our vision everywhere. Tell our employees. Tell our customers. Tell everyone you can. Let's put it on our letterhead and at the top of every report. And we're not only going to promote our vision, we're going to live by it."

Let's take a break and when we come back we can start dealing with the issues. And for each issue we tackle, let's make sure that our decision is inline with our vision." Everyone nodded. It was nice to see Caroline in control. And there was a general feeling that when they came back to discuss the problems they would no longer be just problems. They would seem more like temporary obstacles in the way of achieving their vision.

Andrea sat silently, inconspicuously watching Caroline as she talked. She knew, along with the others, that their new vision wasn't going to solve all of their problems, but it was a start. And more importantly, she once again saw the CEO in Caroline, someone who had a great heart and natural leadership abilities. She also saw someone who was young and inexperienced, so much so that it might imperil the company, but Andrea was willing to take the chance. She had worked for a lot of bad bosses in her day and Caroline wasn't one of them. Caroline was fighting for a cause, something she believed in. It was at that moment that Andrea made up her mind that she believed in it too, and, she believed in Caroline.

Stemming the Tide

Caroline quelled her nervousness as she dialed Reed's number from her office. She had been thinking about this call for much of the weekend. There was only one ring before he was on the other end of the line. "Hello Caroline." Her name had popped up on his Blackberry. "Hello Reed, how was your weekend?" "It was good, good, thanks for asking. But tell me, have you had a chance to think about your action plan yet?"

Caroline politely deflected the question. She thought she might as well get the bad news out of the way quickly so that she could start to make some positive progress. "Reed, just so you know, I learned Saturday night from Andrea that our numbers this month are going to be 30% off our forecast instead of 25%. Left unchecked, that would have increased our burn rate this month by another $45,000." Reed paused before responding. "Well, not a great way to start our Monday morning is it Caroline?" Caroline cringed, but forged on.

"But I want you to know that I've already taken steps to reduce expenses and make up the difference next month so that our cash balance will be on track with the updated budget I presented at the board meeting." Reed came back right at her. "Well, it's good that you're making an adjustment, but both of us know that the real issue is that the top line growth of the company was off another 5%. Something just isn't right. Either the products aren't meeting the demands of the customers or the sales team doesn't know how to sell them or it's something else. Quite frankly, it scares me."

Reed paused for a minute. He didn't want to bring this up, but he liked and respected Caroline and therefore felt he needed to shoot straight. "Caroline, I thought you should know that Mark already sent over to me a resume of a CEO candidate…and he looks pretty good." Caroline's heart dropped and she was glad that she was on the phone so Reed couldn't see her face. "Well, I appreciate you telling me that Reed, but I thought you were going to give me ninety days to turn this thing around?"

"Well, I was, but news like this isn't helping things. Now in reality, this may or may not be the right guy, but even if he is, it would take several weeks to transition him away from his current company. So until then, you have the reigns to show me what you can do."

The good feelings she had after the meeting with her team were now dissipated, but she knew that she had to quickly gather herself. "Reed, why did you invest in UpMarket?" After a momentary pause, he replied, "What do you mean Caroline?" "What I mean is that you invested a lot of money in UpMarket. Although there were probably a few reasons, I'm sure there was something in particular that was compelling. What was it?"

"Well, I thought you had a great idea, a lot of passion and your market is huge." Reed swallowed the hook. "Well, I'm sure that's all right," Caroline answered quickly, "but I'll tell you why you invested in us. You invested in us because you knew that we're going to be so successful that we would provide the software hub, at the center of all digital and interactive media, coordinating the majority of advertisements worldwide." Reed was taken back by what he heard. Here he was talking about replacing Caroline and then she came out with a confident statement like this? He always knew her to be passionate, but now she seemed very directed, even more committed than normal. "Well, I agree. If you phrase it like that, that's exactly why I invested in UpMarket." The discussion lasted a few more minutes and then ended as Reed had to jump on a conference call for another company. After he hung up the phone, Reed wondered, what was that all about? Something was different, something had changed, but he wasn't quite sure what.

Insulation Removed

It was Saturday morning at Starbucks. As usual, Tom already had their lattes waiting in front of their corner chairs. He had a habit of being on time, so much so that he was usually five minutes early. Tom was a classic entrepreneur having started seven companies in his lifetime. Four of them were successful, including his last three start-ups, and his last was his biggest success. He had a great deal of energy and was now restless for something new to work on. Caroline's business problems were the perfect outlet for his passion.

Before Caroline could sit down Tom was already grilling her. "So how did it go this week?" Caroline looked at him and gave him the report. "Well, the good news is that, for all but one member of my management team, they seemed to get it. I was amazed how quickly they grasped the value of having a purpose and vision and, even more than that, contributed to it and embraced the idea. The bad news is that I'm not sure how much longer I'll have my job to be able to make further progress. My investors have already circled the resume of a CEO candidate to take over. It seems that Mark Tobias is the one pushing this new guy the hardest.

Tom thought about it for a minute, paused, and then gave a soft smile. "You know Caroline, it's funny, everyone has a boss. This Mark Tobias probably has pressures of his own from his limited partners expecting a decent return. I can see him getting driven by them as hard as he's driving you. Well, with that said, it just means that we'll have to move a little faster. We have a lot to accomplish. Shall we begin?" Caroline nodded. "Absolutely."

Tom took a sip of his latte. "The next thing we need to develop is unity. Unity is about bringing everyone, the different constituents within your company, together around the major issues that govern the company. This includes shareholders, board, management and employees. You need to evaluate your own beliefs and try to get to the bottom of everyone else's.

Caroline cut in with a grin. "Sounds a little touchy-feely doesn't it?" Tom didn't smile. "Caroline, this is important, and as a matter of fact, it's incredibly relevant to your current situation. For example, you now have a great vision, but if you don't have unity around that vision then you'll never be able to realize it. Lack of unity destroys companies day-in and day-out."

Caroline regretted her impulsive comment. "By unity do you mean like getting John on board with the rest of the management team?" "Exactly. And in terms of John, either on board or out, either way works." Caroline's eyes widened. "Out?! I couldn't fire John. He's obstinate and arrogant, but he knows the systems inside and out, he "controls" the software developers, and he's in charge of the product."

"Well you think that now, but no one is irreplaceable, and if he's not going to be part of the team then he needs to move on. Think of how much time you're wasting dealing with him. We'll get back to that later, but for now, the issue of unity is a much broader issue. Unity is important at many levels including the investor level. Right now this Mark Tobias is not an ally of yours. That's fine. He's entitled to his opinion. But as long as your CEO of this company you need to call him on it. They said that they'd give you ninety days to turn the company around so hold them to their word. Show them that you mean it. Show them that you have a plan. Show them that you're not letting go!"

Caroline was moved by his confidence in her. She was starting to realize why he was so successful. He was good, really good, and they were just getting started. Tom pressed on. "And unity goes much further. Here's what you need to do."

"First, never have different messages for your different constituents. What you say to your shareholders is what you say to your board is the same thing that you say to your employees. Everyone needs to be on the same page. I knew of one company that had financial statements for the board that were the real financial statements, another set for the bank that were more conservative and another set for the employees that were more aggressive. The executives never knew whether they were coming or going or what targets to hit. Everyone needs to play from the same playbook."

"Second, you need unity with your board, which in this case also happens to be the majority of your shareholders. Have you ever sat down with them and discussed how the three of you want the company run? For example, what are their expectations for an exit? I mean when do they expect to sell the company and what valuation would they find reasonable? From what you've told me, it sounds like Reed is a longer-term investor and wants a big win while Mark needs to jazz his portfolio in a hurry and might be fine with something smaller in the near term." Caroline's slow nod showed agreement.

"As you build the company, at what point are they going to want you to start favoring profits over growth? Are either of them biased towards mergers and acquisitions or do they prefer purely internal growth? Are they aligned with how you want to compensate your employees using stock options and possibly even profit sharing?" Caroline cut in. "You know what Tom, over the past year these topics have come up, but only in fragments here and there and always with just Reed or just Mark. I'll be honest, I've never sat everyone down to work through them in a coordinated way." She had an acknowledging look on her face. "Had I done that, I might have able to avoid some of the problems or even surface differences between Reed and Mark that even they didn't know were causing strain on the company. Like their different outlook for an exit."

Tom pushed further. "That's okay, you can start now. And while you're at it, you need to press Mark on the Asics partnership. You've told me yourself that you have too many things going on. You'll never be able to do it all. You need to focus on what's important. And from everything you've told me this far, this partnership isn't even inline with the vision of your company. It's distracting everyone—you, your marketing team and your sales team." Although Tom was telling her something she already knew, she was finally gaining the fortitude to do something about it.

"Caroline, my suggestion is to let your vision provide focus and stop that partnership now and not waste another dollar or man-hour on it. Let Mark know why. Let him see that it's not in the company's best interest. You need to confront Mark on this. At this point, what do you have to lose?" Caroline was getting angry with herself. "Deep down Tom, I always knew that partnership was a distraction. I just didn't have the courage to tell Mark. At first it was just easier to go with the flow, but now I'm really upset with myself and I'm going to fix it."

"Good, decisive steps are what's needed right now. And don't waste time getting upset over things you didn't do in the past. When you've aligned your constituents on issues like these you've achieved unity. Unity enables you do to more with less and make progress faster. It means less time in meetings because everyone's on the same page. It means less politics which creates a healthier environment. While Tom talked, Caroline's determination grew. Why was Mark forcing this partnership on her? Simply to help out one of his other portfolio companies at the expense of UpMarket? That wasn't right and as long as she was CEO she was going to stop it.

Confrontation

It was Monday morning. Caroline was forcing herself to make the dreaded call to Mark. At first she tried to procrastinate with tasks that were suddenly more important, but finally, she decided to just get it over with and give him a call. "Mark, it's Caroline, how are you?" Mark was polite. "Good Caroline, how are you?" "Good. I was hoping you might have some time to get together with me in person this week. There's a few things that I'd like to run by you." Given that he was already out seeking a new CEO, a face-to-face, uncomfortable meeting to discuss her plans for the company wasn't high on his agenda. He didn't bite. "You know Caroline, this week isn't great and I'm traveling all next week. Can we just handle this on the phone?" She knew he was putting her off, but she had to go for it, even if on the phone. Her days might be numbered and she didn't have time to waste.

"Sure," she gave in. "Okay, what's up?" Caroline started speaking passionately about the newly defined vision for the company. She gave him the full story and how the management team, or most of it, was on board too. She was hoping to pull him on board as well, even if it was over the phone. After just a few minutes, she sensed he wasn't engaging with her. Disinterestedly he said, "Sounds good to me." That confirmed to Caroline that she was talking to someone who wasn't listening.

"Okay, well maybe when you get back from your trip we can continue our conversation. It'll be a little easier in person. But there's another item that I need to discuss with you and this one directly concerns you." With that she got his attention. Tentatively she said, "Regarding our relationship with Asics, it's just not working out. I need to end the partnership right away. It's not in line with our core business and where we want to go." Her voice grew stronger. "Most of all it's consuming too much of our software development resources that should only be working on our next release. I know this partnership's important to you, but it's just not working out for UpMarket. Actually, it's hindering us at this point."

There was no immediate response on the other end of the Blackberry. Caroline knew Mark would be upset and braced for the worst. "Caroline! You can't end that partnership. I believe its worthwhile to both UpMarket and Asics. You just haven't given it enough time yet!"

Caroline stood her ground. "Well, I've been speaking with the management team and we're all in agreement. It's just not working out." Immediately, she wished she could have that comment back. Referring to the entire team instead of standing up to Mark alone with her own convictions made her sound like a timid mouse, instead of a CEO. "Caroline, if you end that partnership, then that confirms to me that you just don't have the skills it takes to run this company." Caroline didn't understand the connection. "Mark, I don't think that ending this partnership has anything to do with my CEO skills." Mark snapped back. "Caroline, you're no CEO." Caroline fell back in her chair, dumb-founded. She wasn't new to rude behavior from investors, but she couldn't think of how to respond to this inexcusably hurtful comment. There was only silence. Mark didn't apologize for his outburst. "I'll be calling Reed. I think we need to make a change sooner rather than later."

Pull The Roots

"Reed, it's Mark, do you have a minute?" Reed could tell from the angst in his voice that something was wrong. "What's up Mark?" "Well, it's Caroline. Did you know that she wants to end the partnership with Asics? If it isn't one thing after another. She's really destroying that company. Not only is she burning mountains of cash, she's making it worse everyday that we leave her in charge. I'd like to bring in a new CEO right now. Have you taken a look at that resume I sent over?"

There was a short silence, long enough to tip off Mark that Reed wasn't fully on board with his agenda. "Reed?" Mark prodded. "Ya, I'm still here. I'm just thinking. Mark, she may or may not be the right CEO, but I was never a fan of that partnership either." Mark's tension and anger from his conversation with Caroline had segued right into this one, and was growing, yet he needed to bite his tongue. He needed Reed on his side for the two of them had to be together in the effort to replace Caroline.

"Has Caroline been talking to you about this?" asked Mark. "Actually no. I mean we talked about the company last week, but this subject didn't come up." Mark realized this conversation wasn't yielding what he wanted. He tried another tack. "But, I've already told my partners at Whitepoint that the relationship was solid and that Asics would start to get some traction. I'm sure you can understand." Reed was annoyed. "Mark, this isn't about Asics and your portfolio. Remember, I'm not invested in Asics. This is about UpMarket and what we should do here. And as I said earlier, I can understand why Caroline is doing what she's doing. Now is there anything else?"

Mark was smart enough to stop pushing. Now he was even more upset with Caroline, but it wasn't the time to push the new CEO issue with Reed. Mark abruptly got off the phone. He was consumed with thinking how to bring in a new CEO.

All On The Line

Caroline called another management meeting for Friday morning to review the progress they were making on the operational issues and especially the fate of the next software release. Caroline, John and Deepak had met earlier on the issue, but couldn't come to an agreement on several points. They decided it was better to do a little more investigation on ways to hit the date and then reconvene. One of her goals for this meeting was to reason with John. She knew he could be difficult, but he should certainly be committed to the company. He had a lot of stock options in UpMarket and a lot of time and effort invested as well. She thought she might be able to pull him on board. She really needed a tight, unified management team to tackle problems together and push the company forward.

"Okay everyone, let's start the meeting and find out how we're doing. Andrea, can you fill everyone in on how the numbers look?" Andrea sorted her papers in front of her, although it was more of a habit since she always knew the numbers cold. "Sure. They're not pretty, but here they are. Our revenues for June were $630,000 which is about

30% below our projection of $900,000. Our expenses were just a little over $900,000, so including some equipment purchases, we burned another $300,000. Our cash balance is $1.9 million." The group began to ask Andrea a number of questions about the financials, but since the questions were mostly about revenues, after a few minutes, she passed the baton on to Keith. "Keith, can you take over?"

He started his overview with an update on Pepsi so he could be the owner of some good news. "I've contacted Pepsi and they've given us a date so we can get out there and present them our plan." Caroline understood that this was a big opportunity. She had reviewed the plan and knew it was good. "Caroline, we're going to put the plan in presentation form and we'll have something for you in just a day or two." "Looking forward to it!" Caroline's response was a little over enthusiastic, but she welcomed the good news. After that, Keith gave a short rundown of the top ten sales prospects and then the conversation went over to Beth.

Caroline led the inquisition. "Beth, how are we doing?" Beth looked uncomfortable, too many sleepless nights in her eyes. "We've taken Sandy off the Pepsi account. She just wasn't seasoned enough. So we're making progress there, but we're having a hard time with some of the other accounts and keeping up with the Call Center volume." Andrea jumped in. "I hear that some of our new people are giving bad information causing frustrated customers and multiple call backs." Beth was defensive. "Some of that did happen Andrea, but I think we've taken steps to fix that. I should have a better feel for it come Monday when we compile this week's call statistics." Caroline let her off the hook. "Okay, let us know what you find."

It was time to steer the conversation to John. Caroline knew it might be contentious, so she took a breath to make sure that her voice didn't reflect any unease. "John, how are we coming with the release? Have you been able to figure out how to make up the lost time?" John was silent for an awkward moment, but then responded in a detached way. "Not really.

What we found after digging a little more is that the product requirements from Marketing weren't fully fleshed out and there's a lot more development than we anticipated." Deepak responded sharply and defensively. "What do you mean John? You've known the requirements for four months now. It's just the way that you've chosen to implement the code that's costing us the delay. Why not just develop it to suit this release and then next time we'll factor in more time so that you can develop more "leveragible" code. And while we're at it, why not shelve your licensed software project for the time being so you can throw all you've got at the release?"

By now, John was seething. He had been waiting for this and his anger went from zero to ballistic with that one comment. "Deepak, we do that all the time! I'm tired of building spaghetti code. It's time to start doing things properly around here. And in terms of the licensed software initiative, don't go there."

Caroline tried to calm both of them. She mustered up all of her internal resources to keep emotions out of it and focus on the real issue rather than get caught between the normal battle fire between marketing and development. "John, Deepak, let's look at the bigger picture here. This isn't so much about who has the better solution to the problem, but the fact that there's a lot riding on this release. Our investors don't want to hear that we've missed yet another date, and more importantly, our customers are waiting for the auto-optimization release and we really need it to start generating sales. Last month we missed our sales targets by 30% and we can't do that again. We've got to start closing the gap. Can't we just agree that this month we'll take the fastest route to solve the problem, get the release out on time, and then from this point on build in enough time into our release dates so that we can develop the software in the best way possible?"

John wasn't buying the compromise. "Caroline, we always do that and the treadmill has got to stop. We always say next time, next time, and this time I have to put my foot down." And this time, Caroline thought, John had gone over the edge. She didn't like the fact that her fate at UpMarket was potentially in his hands. She needed to start rebuilding her credibility with the board, and one more missed date would be the final straw in her demise. She tried to appeal to John in a calmer voice. "John, I know you're frustrated, but the right move for the team is to finish the release, get it out on time, and start generating those sales that we know are out there. Don't you agree?"

"No!" he shouted. "I'm tired of this. I'm tired of us not hitting our numbers. I'm tired of our competitors pushing past us all the time. It's time to make a change." John knew that Caroline was in a precarious position. And, frustrated for months, he picked now as the time to make his stand. Protocol and deference were gone. Caroline could feel that she was losing control, the situation escalating from bad to worse. John went on. "Caroline, if we do it as you say, it's going to send the wrong message to my entire software development team. I can't tolerate that anymore. You'd have to find a new CTO."

Caroline was sitting on the edge of her chair leaning forward. She was trying to remain calm but the tension was getting the better of her and it was creeping into her face. She couldn't believe it was *now* that he chose to make his stand. He not only questioned her authority in front of the entire management team, but at a time when she had very little credibility with the board. She had so many things running through her mind and she was subconsciously calculating them all in an instant. In that brief moment, time seemed to stop.

Then it clicked. She knew what she had to do and that it had to be done now. Caroline always took ownership of whatever she committed to and because of that, she knew intuitively that her response shouldn't be what would help her save her job, but to do what was right for the company. She had always held a steadfast resolve to do whatever it took to make the company succeed.

Now there was only one move in her mind. Even if she was asked to leave the company because of it, she could hold her head high. She was going to make the right decision for the right reasons. And she wasn't going to make excuses or provide rationalizations to Reed and Mark. She would come right out and tell them what was going on. She wasn't afraid of the consequences anymore. She had agonized long enough over losing the CEO role. She was tired of it.

When she spoke, her calmness was surprising. "John, actually I don't want to find a new CTO, but if you don't hit the release date with the plan that the team suggests, I will find a new CTO." Normally she would ask John to meet privately before making such a comment, but he had forced her into a public battle and she wasn't going to shirk from it.

John was shocked. He had miscalculated that Caroline had no where to turn and would back down. Instead, it was he who was cornered. "Okay, then I guess I'm done here." His comment was intended to be a slight opportunity for her to give him an out, but Caroline didn't bite. Now John's anger grew as reality set in. He wanted desperately to show her she had made a mistake. All he could do was to throw a weak jab at her. "Looks like your software release is never going to make it out the door now." Caroline didn't hesitate. "That's fine John, we'll work it out."

In the aftermath of the battle Caroline was at first satisfied with her pyrrhic victory, but then it set in that she might have uttered her last official directive as CEO. The management team was stunned. On the one hand, the swiftness of what just happened seemed like a reckless move. Was the company falling apart before their eyes? On the other hand, they felt relief. John had always been difficult, it was time for a change and they were impressed that Caroline had had the backbone to take him head on, especially publicly. Caroline's mind was racing. Now, not only would they not make the release date, but she had to communicate to the board that her CTO had just resigned. Could things get any worse?

Real Doubt

This time Caroline beat Tom to Starbucks. It was a busy Saturday morning crowded with spectators from a 20k race up the road. Their normal meeting spot wasn't available so she took the only open table close to the queue of people waiting for their coffees. Rather than the comfortable, velvet armchairs, she was stuck with the hard, heavy, unbreakable sentinels that had served thousands of customers. She was frustrated enough as it was and now was more irritated that everyone would overhear her conversation with Tom.

She sat down without getting the lattes so she wouldn't lose the last table available. She daydreamed while she waited. She hadn't noticed before but the colorful drawing on the chalk board was obviously done by an artist. She wondered if it was done by a local employee or someone at the corporate office. Then she realized everything else in the store was perfectly designed and coordinated. From the cash register to the espresso bar there was a broad array of colors, tile and artwork. The open top shelving displayed ground coffee, teas and flavoring syrups while the bottom shelves offered espresso machines for purchase. Everything was in its place and they were efficiently serving dozens of customers every hour. She wished UpMarket was that well organized.

"Hello Caroline! How's it going?" In the middle of her daydream, Tom came up from behind and startled her when he tapped her on the shoulder. Caroline didn't offer her normal smile. She didn't even offer a hello. She looked him right in the eye and said, "Tom, I'm in a real mess. I'm not so sure this is working." Tom sat down suppressing his intense need for a latte. "What do you mean?" Caroline took a breath to compose her thoughts.

"Where should I start? I spoke with Mark about ending the partnership with Asics and he was mad, really mad. When the conversation ended, he was going to call Reed to fire me officially and make finding a new CEO a priority. Then in my management meeting, my CTO openly confronted me. He sort of resigned and I sort of fired him. Anyway, he's gone and now we're not going to hit the release date. I have a customer meeting coming up with Pepsi and we really need the release as part of our plan to get them re-engaged. They've been delayed enough. We can't tell them yet again, 'It's coming.' We simply need to deliver it. Let's just say, it hasn't been a very good week."

She couldn't understand why Tom didn't look upset as well. Why was he smiling? Didn't he realize that her career was on the line? She looked down so she wouldn't say something she would regret. Tom tried to get her attention. "Hey," he said softly. She didn't budge. "Caroline, look at me please. This isn't necessarily that bad." Caroline's head shot up. "What do you mean? How can you say this isn't that bad?" "Well, let's think about it. You were on your way out the door before any of this happened. It was evident that you needed to shake things up a bit. If it were up to John you were going to miss that release date anyway. And, everything you did was an attempt to create unity among your investors and management team. Unity that was sorely missing. So from my point of view, even if you do get asked to leave, those were the right moves. You were providing leadership. Leadership that hadn't been there before."

Caroline thought about it. "I know, but these guys are pretty rough, there's no need for some of the things they said." Tom sympathized. "Yes, but unfortunately, sometimes that's the way these things work when you bring investors on board. Millions of dollars, people's reputations, and people's livelihoods are all at stake. Sometimes the powers-that-be can come in and trample all over things before they get them smoothed out.

For the moment, Caroline wished she could start over. Return the money and go back to the day when she had just ten employees. "You know, all I tried to do was build a company that could provide great products for our customers and was a great place to work. Look at where I am now. It's not what I planned." Tom seized the opportunity. "Caroline, I don't want to see you get hurt, but whatever you do, don't check your ideals at the door. Keep them intact, that's your most powerful asset as CEO. What we really need to do is get this business performing. That's the only way that you'll gain control of your own fate."

Tom knew that her situation was going to get worked out one way or another. A lack of unity, especially amongst the board members or management team, would get resolved one way or another. And the current crisis was going to provide the impetus. The strongest power, the one with the most influence, or the one with the most equity, or the one with the most money, would surface and the others would either fall inline or leave the company. When it came to difficult members on a management team, he knew that the best thing to do was to get them in line fast or ask them to leave. They brought down the rest of the staff and created more problems than good. And, this rule went for the rock star contributors, like John, as well. In this case, now he was gone, and the company could move forward again.

Dealing with Mark was a much more difficult issue, Tom thought. You just don't ask an investor to leave your company. Sure, in some cases, you might try to buy them out, but no one was going to invest in UpMarket at this point and who knows what Mark would ask for even if he did want to get out.

Caroline reflected for a minute. "I guess that's just what I was doing. I've got to tell you, as it was all going on, I was pretty nervous." Tom laughed. "Why does everyone think that leaders are these brave unemotional people? I think leaders just seem to hide their feelings a little better, that's all." Caroline laughed too and released some of her tension. "I guess so." Tom had calmed her down. "How about I get us a couple of lattes and we talk through this a bit more?" Caroline nodded. "That'd be great."

Before Tom rose to get the lattes, he snapped his fingers. "Caroline, before I forget, please make a note for our next meeting. Be prepared to talk about everything you know about your market, customers, products, competitors, suppliers, people, processes and distribution capabilities. All the core activities of your business. I'm sure you've done something like this for the investor meetings in the past." Caroline pulled out a pen and made the note. As she was writing she thought that it sounded like heavy stuff and wanted to know more. "Why, what are we going to talk about?" As Tom walked towards the coffee line he said, "You'll see."

A Bright Spot In Development

"Caroline, you wanted to see me?" It was Jake Porter knocking on Caroline's open office door. Jake was the number two developer behind John Chen. As Caroline's very first employee he knew the software better than anyone. At 25, he was young, but with the polar opposite of John's personality. He had been Caroline's original choice for the CTO job, but Reed and Mark felt he was too unseasoned, so John was brought in as a condition of their investment. John's style had been to tell the team what to do and he didn't tolerate any questions. Jake, however, liked to include his team in decisions and let them know why they were being made. He felt they responded better when they were given all the facts.

"Hey Jake, come on in." Caroline waved at him. "It's pretty obvious that John's left and I wanted to talk about it with you." Jake was a little uncomfortable talking about his "former" boss of only twelve hours. What if John came back? Or would he soon have a new boss? A lot was going through his mind. "Well, we're all going to miss John. He was here for a long time and we all know how good he was. But we'll manage. I know the software pretty well and the guys are in decent spirits." That was an understatement. There were many software developers who were quite pleased, even elated, to discover John was gone.

Caroline read Jake's face as he spoke. "Jake, you and I have known each other for a long time now. There's a void that we have to fill with John gone and I want you to take the acting-CTO role. Do you think you can do it?" Jake was visibly blown away. "Me? I didn't think you were going to consider me for that position based on what happened last year when you brought John in." Caroline understood his confusion at the turn of events. "That was a different time and under different circumstances. I know how passionate you are about this company and our products and I know that everyone in the company really likes you and respects you. So how about we do this. I'll give you the acting-CTO title and we'll see how you do. If all goes well after a couple of months, we'll make it official and give you the full CTO title. Sound good?"

Jake tried to contain himself. "Sounds great. And by the way, Caroline, I won't let you down. I want that job and we're going to build one hell of a release. And, I think I know of a couple of things we can do to make the release get out on time. Let me get together with the team and I'll let you know if it's doable. Okay?"

Caroline was already convinced she had made the right moves. "Absolutely. Let's talk tomorrow. And, by the way, don't you think it makes sense to suspend that licensed software initiative?" Jake smiled knowingly. "You bet Caroline. For starters, it's not in line with our vision." Caroline smiled. Not just because he wanted to suspend the initiative too, but because he called it 'our vision'."

Caroline needed to call both Reed and Mark and bring them up to speed on John and now Jake. First on her list was Mark. While she didn't like approaching a rattlesnake while its tail was still rattling, there was a definite advantage to getting it over with. If nothing else, she didn't want to live in fear of her fate. She'd rather just know and take the suspense out of it. She dialed Mark, but he didn't answer, so she left him a voicemail. Perhaps he was screening her calls to avoid her.

Her next call was to Reed. Caroline knew that keeping Reed informed, communicating frequently and honestly, was the only way to work through her situation. She happened to catch him in the office. They talked for a little while about John and her backup plan with Jake. As it turned out, the conversation went quite well. To her surprise, over the past year, Reed had witnessed John in action and realized that he didn't like him very much because he thought he wasn't a team player. And he liked Jake's enthusiastic embrace of the position and the possibility that the release might come out on time.

"Caroline, my wife and I are going to South America for two weeks and I'll be hard to reach. Keep pushing, get that release out, and let's catch up as soon as I get back. Okay?" Caroline felt a new warmth in his seemingly supportive comment, but whether it was truly intended or even there at all, she wasn't sure. Yet, gratefully, she grabbed it and held it with both hands. "Sounds good Reed, I look forward to hearing about your trip. Enjoy and see you soon." Caroline's eyes squinted as she thought hard. Now she had an inside track developing. A few weeks respite to try and sort things out. Reed was out of town and Mark wasn't actively seeking her out. Finally, she had some time to maneuver.

Liberation

The next morning Jake let Caroline know that after speaking with his team they all felt confident that they could rally and meet the release date. Ecstatic, Caroline immediately called the management team together to make sure all systems were go. This was going to be a true team effort and all departments needed to be coordinated to make sure it went off without a hitch. Deepak, Keith, Beth and Andrea filed into the conference room to join Jake and Caroline. The buzz that the release was back on track had already started to spread throughout the company.

"Jake, before we begin the meeting, I'd just like to give you a round of applause for finding a way to make this happen." Caroline started to clap and everyone around the table immediately joined in. Jake was a little embarrassed, but it felt good to be recognized. Deepak was curious. "What did you have to do to make sure we could hit the date?" "Well, we know we've only got six days to make it happen. So we have no choice but to cut out a few steps from the release process. But, the good news is that a majority of this stuff has already been through quality assurance, so what we really need to focus on is the remaining QA, fixing any final bugs we find, and then put all of our efforts into the release process. The key was suspending the licensed software project because two critical Release Engineers were tied up with that. The team knows how important this is and they're going to make sure it happens."

It was refreshing for Caroline to have a CTO that was trying to make things happen rather than present obstacles. What a difference. "Okay everyone, let's run through this and make sure that we're all on the same page. Deepak. Is your team ready to go?" "We are. We're just crossing t's and dotting some i's, but we'll be ready. The new release email explaining all of the updates is going out today and then one more time right before the release. We have a press release already written. Once you review it and sign off, that'll be ready to go out the day of the release. All-in-all we're in pretty good shape."

"Great, how about your team Keith?" "My guys will be blown away. They all thought this release was a lost cause and didn't have a snowball's-chance-in-hell of getting out. They've all been trained on the new features, ad nauseam, know what to say to the customers, and quite frankly, just can't wait to start selling." Momentum was building. It's always motivating to hear your VP of Sales get pumped up.

"Andrea, how about your group?" "Well, we have it easy on this release. Deepak and I made sure in the product requirements that none of the billing information would change. That way when the auto-optimization occurs, it should be just better results for the customers and more revenue for us. The bills should go out as normal. The electronic billing innovation we put in place when I first started here has been a Godsend. So I'm happy just to watch it all happen!"

Caroline completed the circle of questions with Beth. "Okay Beth, that leaves the hard stuff to you." Beth accepted the fact that Customer Service always got the raw end of the deal when it came to new releases, but she secretly enjoyed the fact that when the whistle blew it was her team on the field. "Ya, we'll expect a lot of calls at first. No matter how well the release goes and how good the documentation is, customers typically just don't read it. They call instead. The good news is that everyone's trained and ready to go. We did a smart thing by having the Customer Service Reps help out with a lot of the QA so they're pretty familiar with the release. We'll keep an eye on the call volume and some of the guys on Jake's team said they'd help out if it get's too crazy."

Caroline felt it all coming together. They were about to pull a victory out of the ashes. "Nice job everyone. Sounds like we're going to pull this off after all." Jake interrupted her before she could adjourn the meeting.

"Just one more thing Caroline. When I was talking with my team about getting this release out on time, I told them that the importance for speed wasn't just about this release, but about all future releases as well. I described to them how it was back when we first started and how fast we moved then." Caroline and the entire team where intrigued by the comments of their new management team cohort. Caroline was interested in how he characterized the early days. "What did you say?"

"I told them that with only $50,000 in seed money, we always approached everything we did with a mindset of 'no money, no access, no time.' Essentially, the best innovations don't necessarily stem from the biggest budgets with the most people and resources. Ironically, they often come from the tiniest budgets and smallest teams and individuals. In those situations, you need to be fast, you need to be creative, you need to do things differently. Well, the guys started asking more and more questions. I told them how it was when it was just you and I and how fast we could move. You'd verbally tell me what the software needed to do and then I just took it from there and coded. The two of us were the product research, product requirements, architects, developers, QA and release people all rolled into a tight two-person team. So one of my guys said, "Well if that's what generates speed and results, then why don't we just try to recreate that?" And that got me thinking. Here's what I'd like to propose."

Everyone was amazed at Jake's newfound confidence. They could tell this guy was serious about keeping the CTO role. He was aggressive and wanted to make his mark, but he was also acting very much like a team player, even a leader. "Deepak, here's what I'd love to try and pull off. I'd like to present this new process at our next monthly Innovation Meeting. In preparation, let's get your team and my team together and work through the entire development process, from start to finish. We both know we need good customer research, tight product requirements, good development practices and solid QA. However, let's try to cut out every other unnecessary email, document, meeting, and interaction possible. I mean let's jettison everything that isn't absolutely unnecessary. Let's not only create results, let's create pure speed. We'll call it speed development or something like that." Deepak was all over it. "Jake, just say when and we'll make it happen. We'll make it part of our competitive advantage and call it Need-for-Speed Development." Everyone smiled. Deepak always had to put a marketing slant on everything.

The team adjourned. With John gone and the new, enthusiastic influence of Jake, it was probably the best team meeting that they'd had in over a year. Everyone was working together for the common cause and it felt good.

Chiseling Through

Every year Tom vacationed on Nantucket for two weeks at the end of July. It had been a beautiful summer so far and he got lucky with the weather. However, by the end of the second week he had grown restless and began to think more and more about UpMarket. Days in the sun without one of his own businesses to occupy his thoughts had created a void in his mind easily filled by UpMarket.

During that time Caroline spent a great deal of time on the road with her clients, especially Pepsi. She spent three days onsite with them personally working with each member of the client's team. It was an opportunity to teach them about the intricacies of online advertising as well as the more advanced capabilities of UpMarket's systems. After her visit, they were fully engaged and especially impressed with the auto-optimization release that Jake had managed to get out on time.

As Caroline greeted Tom at their first Starbucks get-together since his vacation, she realized she missed these meetings. Things were improving at UpMarket and it was a relief to have their largest customer back on track, but still something wasn't quite right. And she couldn't figure out what it was. After catching up for a few minutes, Caroline explained why she was puzzled.

"Tom, I'm not sure what's wrong. Our release has been out for a couple of weeks now and our revenues have climbed a little as a result, but I'm not seeing the significant impact I expected. And what's hanging over my head like a cleaver is the fact that we're down to $1.6 million in cash. I've talked with Keith to see what he and the sales team thinks. They're saying everyone's on vacation and it's just a slow time of year, but I don't buy it. We should be seeing better results by now."

"Caroline, I've wanted to get to this for a while and it's regarding the note I had you make at our last meeting. I thought a lot about it over my vacation. You and I never dug into your business model to make sure it's still working the way you expect it to work. Your market changes so rapidly that it's easy for it to get out-of-synch. Let's stop for a moment and go back. Describe your business model in detail for me." Caroline thought for a minute and realized that although she'd talked about her business model countless times before, she had never been asked to describe it in detail.

She paused to think about Tom's question. "Well, our clients are major advertisers across the country. They pay us to place their ads on the websites of publishers who are part of our ad network. Essentially, we're selling the banner and video ad inventory of our publisher's websites. We make our money by taking a percentage of the rate charged to the advertiser as a commission and the rest goes back to the publisher." She finished and looked to him for his approval. Tom tilted his head. "That's it?" Caroline shrugged as if to say yes. "Caroline, that's your revenue model, not your full business model."

Caroline was uneasy. How could she be the CEO of a software startup, having raised $6 million, and not really know what a business model was? What was she missing? What was he looking for? Whenever someone asked her about her business model that was the answer she gave them. And plenty of other CEOs talked the same way. Did she have all those conversations without really understanding what she was talking about? Did others do the same?

"Tom, what else are you looking for?" Tom knew that she didn't fully understand the critical concept. "Let me explain. As we go through this, keep in mind that people smarter than me write volumes about this stuff and can make it very complicated. But for me, I like to keep things simple and straightforward. In fact, that's the key, the more straightforward the better."

"First, every CEO needs to have a clear picture of their business model because it defines how their company makes money." Caroline spoke up. "That's it? Isn't that's what I told you? How we get paid." Tom shook his head. "Not exactly. A business model describes the value that you give to your customers, that's what you described, but it also describes *how you deliver that value.* The value you give generates revenue and how you deliver it creates expenses. The difference is your profit." Caroline quipped, "Or in our case, lack of profit." Tom grinned. "Right, we'll be getting to that later."

"A long time ago I created this template to help me structure a business model. It'll help you." Tom handed Caroline a copy of the template. As Caroline was reviewing it he went on.

Business Model

A. Quantify the specific value that you provide to your customers:

<u>Market.</u> Clearly and narrowly define the set of customers that you sell to regularly. Is that market emerging, growing, maturing or declining?

_____
_____
_____
_____
_____

<u>Customer.</u> Do you understand your customer's specific problems and needs? Why do they prefer your products or services over your competitors?

_____
_____
_____
_____
_____

<u>Products, Services.</u> Does your solution provide enough value so that your customers pay reasonably for it?

_____
_____
_____
_____
_____

<u>Competitors.</u> How do they make money? Are they winning business? Why?

_____
_____
_____
_____
_____

<u>Revenue Model.</u> One-time sales, monthly subscription, per transaction? Complimentary revenue streams?

_____
_____
_____
_____
_____

Business Model

B. Quantify how you provide that value to your customers:

<u>Raw Goods</u>. Do you have a cost advantage or access advantage from your suppliers?

_____

_____

_____

_____

<u>People</u>. Do you have the right people for your model? How does your talent compare with that of the competition?

_____

_____

_____

_____

<u>Processes</u>. How do you design, build, fulfill and service your product? What are your capabilities such as break-through technologies, patents, brands, quality levels or service levels?

_____

_____

_____

_____

<u>Distribution</u>. Is it wider? Faster? Eliminated? Partners?

_____

_____

_____

_____

<u>Expense Model</u>. How do you allocate your resources? Do you spend more in certain areas that you feel resonate more with your clients?

_____

_____

_____

_____

"The business model is at the core of your company and it's what generates your cash flow. Keep in mind that more than one company can share a business model, even an entire industry, but how that model is implemented can vary widely and so do the resulting profits. Every component of the business model fuses with the others to create the bottom line. Another way to say it is that every company has the same "ingredients" of a business model, but the recipe of how you mix them and in what quantities creates a different outcome and differentiates your company. And remember that there're always tradeoffs. For example, if you're seeking higher margins you'll likely need to be more unique and that'll require more investment. But if you're successful, the benefits outweigh the costs."

"Tom, I like this template. It's simple, and it makes you think about the most important components of your business in relation to one other." "That's right Caroline. Let's test it out. Why not use the template and see if you can walk me through UpMarket's business model again."

"Let's see. Starting with the value that we provide our customers. Our market is online advertising. Fortunately, it's pretty hot. Online banner advertising is growing 35% a year and online video advertising is growing 120% a year." She was talking aloud as she looked down at the template. "My customers want control over their brand and to know that their ads are being displayed on reputable websites. And in a perfect world, they would rather work with just one company that could get them to any website, rather than work with multiple vendors. That way their reporting could be standardized. And they prefer UpMarket's services because we provide the largest ad network and all the websites are vetted thoroughly—they're getting quality. Our pricing is fair—we're not the most expensive and not the cheapest either. When it comes to our competitors, they're maneuvering constantly. Some of them aren't getting traction, but others are gaining on us."

Tom stopped her. "Why are some doing well?" Caroline pondered the question for a moment. "Well, Xenic Systems is the market leader and does okay. It's because they've got a decent product and decent service and they're reliable. Although, their ad network has holes and they lose a fair number of deals to us because of it. Marlin Networks really doesn't have a competitive offering, but they just landed GM." Tom looked a little surprised. "If it's not competitive then how could they land GM? Isn't that a pretty big deal?" Caroline nodded. "It is a big deal, but they landed it because one of their board members is good friends with one of the execs in charge of the GM account." Tom shrugged. "Ahhhh. Happens to the best of us."

Caroline went on. "One competitor in particular, Miami Media, just raised another $10 million in addition to their original $5 million and they seem to be everywhere lately. Deep pockets really help." Tom wanted more. "Sure, money always helps, but usually there's some other reason why they're gaining." Caroline confirmed his suspicion. "It's because they're so new with a brand new infrastructure and they're focusing on video ads only. It doesn't compare well to our broader offering of both banner ads and video ads, but they sure do a great job with video so if that's all a customer needs then they stack up well." Tom nodded thoughtfully. He was taking in all of the competitive positioning.

"Caroline, that's all good. I particularly like the fact that we've got a hot market. We just need to get UpMarket's profits..." He stopped himself and winked at Caroline. "...I mean future profits growing more quickly than the market. When we do that, it means we've developed a sustainable competitive advantage. Now tell me how you *provide* the value to your customers."

Caroline went to the next page of the template. "We really don't have any raw goods from suppliers, but we do have great people, especially those who have been with me the longest. They're all fantastic at what they do and some have even helped shape the industry as it's evolved. Regarding processes, whether its coding systems, servicing customers, managing our operations center or whatever, we focus on speed, creativity and experimentation. We're just natural innovators when it comes to that stuff. And in terms of distribution, I think our ad network would fall into this category. We have the largest ad network in the industry. As far as our expense model goes, we leverage PR heavily. We think it's a credible way to position ourselves as the technology market leader. And, we invest a considerable amount in training, much more than our competitors. Our customers really feel that our customer service people are the most knowledgable in the industry. In fact, that goes for our sales people and almost everyone in our company..."

Tom looked at Caroline. As she uttered those words, her speech had slowed, and then stopped altogether. Frozen for a moment, she looked at Tom. "That's it!" "What?" Tom caught her eyes, now shining with realization. "That's what's wrong with my business model!" Tom pleaded. "Well, then tell me!"

Caroline described her revelation. "Early on, before we received any venture funding, we were a tight team. I only had ten people and we all knew how to do almost every job at the company. We were all interacting with customers and each one of us became experts in online advertising. It didn't matter if one of us was in customer support, software development or sales. Our customers knew that we provided more than just technology, we provided knowledge about a very new and evolving industry. And, because everyone was on the front lines, we were learning massive amounts in real-time. We became known as the innovators and experts. Then two things happened. First, we got the funding, and my company grew from ten people to sixty. We made our hires as fast as we could, and even though we felt they were smart, great people, many were new to the industry. The result was that one of the real differentiators that set us apart, our expertise, had been dramatically watered down. And then to make matters worse, about six months ago, since we weren't hitting our revenue targets, we cut the training budget to ease the burn rate. That compounded the problem even more! We had all these new people and we weren't spending any time training them!"

"Caroline, it sounds like you might have figured it out. That's very plausible." Caroline was thrilled by her discovery.

"You were the one who got me there." For the next hour, they delved deeper and deeper into business models—both UpMarket's and the competitors'—in search of what was working in the industry and what wasn't. Caroline was gaining an intimate understanding of each competitor's strengths and weaknesses, how they were differentiating, and how they attempted to stand out in front of the customer. By the end of their meeting, Tom knew she was excited, but wanted to temper her enthusiasm just a bit. "It looks like we've figured out a piece to the puzzle, haven't we?" Caroline smiled in acknowledgment. "The only thing to keep in mind is that this is a rather big puzzle with a lot of small pieces. If you can solve the training issue, I fully expect it'll have a solid impact, but there's a lot to do, so don't expect it to solve all your problems. Okay?" Caroline knew where Tom was going with his comment. "I know Tom, there's no magic bullet, but this was a big realization."

Caroline reflected on Tom's caution. First, how quickly could she solve this problem and how much could she expect it to impact revenue? And even more importantly, if she was just discovering this oversight, what else hadn't she seen and how would she find out?

Spot Check

Caroline was energized to solve the training problem and move on. She knew she was on to something, but she wanted to bounce the idea off someone on her management team for an "inside" confirmation. Andrea seemed the obvious choice. Her CFO could easily cut through the smoke, was very analytical, but even more importantly, Caroline knew she'd tell it like it was. Caroline called her to see if she could meet for coffee on Sunday morning at the Public Garden. Andrea could hear the excitement in Caroline's voice and was intrigued to know what she had found.

On Sunday they found a vacant, wood bench by the swan boats in the Garden. It was a beautiful summer day to relax, but these days they found themselves working every day. "Andrea, I found a critical flaw in our business model. Tell me what you think." Caroline took about fifteen minutes to get Andrea through the business model and her discovery. She passionately explained the model, flipped through the template and barely took a breath. Andrea followed closely and got it every step of the way.

"Caroline, I've gotta say I'm impressed." Caroline smiled. She took that for agreement. "Thanks Andrea, I was shocked when I realized how critical our training was too." Andrea corrected her. "No. What I mean is that I agree with what you found, but I'm impressed at your tenacity. You're not letting this go! It's really comforting to know how much you care and that you're going to make this work, no matter what it takes." Caroline was moved. She hadn't expected that comment. "Hey thanks Andrea, I really appreciate that."

They finished their coffee while talking over details of the plan. After an hour, Andrea left and Caroline sat alone pondering her thoughts. Andrea's reaction was very gratifying, and the next step was to run it by her full management team, but, she wondered, how much of an impact could she expect from solving this one problem? Would it be enough to get the company back on track?

Course Correction

Caroline couldn't wait to get started. She asked her management team to get in the office by 8:00am on Monday. There was a lot to cover and no time to waste. Everyone arrived on time, coffee in hand, eager to learn what she had found. Step-by-step, she took them through the business model template that her "friend" had given her and showed them the glaring flaw. Everyone agreed that the lack of training was a major problem. It was so simple that they were bothered that they hadn't noticed it before. In the middle of the chaos, distracted by everyday issues, they hadn't seen the longer-term effects of some of their decisions. It took the business model template to identify it. Energy seeped into the room because they not only found the problem, but they knew they could fix it.

Beth spoke up. "You know, it all makes sense now. It's the same thing that happened with Pepsi, isn't it? When we landed all those accounts earlier this year, I had to transfer some of our best people off Pepsi and on to the others. I had to spread everyone out and eventually I ran out of experienced people to put on accounts. It was the inexperienced replacements that got us in trouble. I know we've corrected the Pepsi situation, but it's a systemic problem on all accounts. I subconsciously knew it wasn't right, but we were moving too fast to stop, take the time, and do something about it."

Caroline made another point. "You're right Beth. And not only do well-trained people impact customer service, they impact revenues as well. Just like when I was with Pepsi, if you can effectively communicate your solutions to your clients and solve their problems, then naturally they're going to use your service more. Our new people just weren't engaging the clients—they didn't know how!"

"Listen everyone." Andrea broke in. "I have an idea. We're saving about $30,000 by skipping that tradeshow with Asics. We were going to pocket the savings, but what if we redirected it instead and spent it on more training? Let's face it, there couldn't be a better way to allocate those dollars. That's what's going to support our revenues." No one hesitated and no discussion was needed. It was the right move.

For the next two hours the team went back and forth, arguing and then finally agreeing on the details of their business model. And then they compared their model to their competitors to draw distinctions, determine what was working in their industry and what wasn't. Andrea took notes and filled out the template as they developed it. Once they were done, she printed copies for another review.

UpMarket
Business Model

A. Quantify the specific value that you provide to your customers:

Market. Clearly and narrowly define the set of customers that you sell to regularly. Is that market emerging, growing, maturing or declining?

Our market is narrowly defined as those customers requiring placement of online banner ads and rich media video ads across a wide variety of website publishers. In 2006, banner advertising is a $16b market growing 35%+ annually and rich media video advertising is a $640m market growing 120% annually.

Customer. Do you understand your customer's specific problems and needs? Why do they prefer your products or services over your competitors?

Online advertising is a nascent and evolving industry. Our customers want: 1) our expertise to help them with their online campaigns; 2) the highest response rates possible; 3) control over where their brand is viewed and only on reputable websites; 4) standardized reporting across vendors.

Products, Services. Does your solution provide enough value so that your customers pay reasonably for it?

Our solution provides: 1) senior UpMarket personnel that are knowledgeable and experienced; 2) respectable response rates; 3) the largest and highest quality ad network; 4) compliance with industry standard reporting.

Competitors. How do they make money? Are they winning business? Why?

Xenic Systems: Market leader. Cash flow breakeven. Product and service are decent. Solid customer base. Revenue model same, but charge higher commission rates. Network quality is weak point.

Marlin Networks: Weak product and service. in building stage. very aggressive. Other than GM as a marquee customer, they have few other big names. Revenue model same as ours although lower pricing. Ad network is smaller. They focus on advertising over product development.

Miami Media: Recent $10m capital raise on top of initial $5m. Heavy focus on video ads and no capability for banner ads. New infrastructure. newly developed software, clean slate. Niche capabilities.

Revenue Model. One-time sales, monthly subscription, per transaction? Complimentary revenue streams?
Commission-based revenue model based on click-through transactions only. Commission rate of 7% to 15% of publisher banner ad rates and 20% to 45% of publisher video ad rates.

UpMarket
Business Model

B. Quantify how you provide that value to your customers:

<u>Raw Goods</u>. Do you have a cost advantage or access advantage from your suppliers?

Being a software company, we don't have any "raw goods" in our model.

<u>People</u>. Do you have the right people for your model? How does your talent compare with that of the competition?

Our longest tenured employees are some of the best in the business (65% have an advertising or technology background versus a projected 40% at our biggest competitor). They are certainly the most knowledgeable when it comes to online advertising. However, our staff has grown 500% over the past year and now many of our people are new to the business.

<u>Processes</u>. How do you design, build, fulfill and service your product? What are your capabilities such as break-through technologies, patents, brands, quality levels or service levels?

Our engineers are U.S. based and in Boston. Xenic Systems off-shores the majority of their development at a lower cost. We have 3 patents-pending which aren't expected to be approved for 2 years. We focus on innovation to lead the industry and improve our internal operations. We're focusing heavily on providing knowledgeable customer service.

<u>Distribution</u>. Is it wider? Faster? Eliminated? Partners?

Our website network is the largest in the industry. In addition to being the largest, we believe that our website publishers are of the highest quality. Our publishers must pass a 10-point Quality Assessment test before being included in the network. This resonates with our clients that want to know that their ads are being displayed in reputable locations.

<u>Expense Model</u>. How do you allocate your resources? Do you spend more in certain areas that you feel resonate more with your clients?

We leverage PR heavily as a credible way to position ourselves as the innovation market leader. A portion of our advertising dollars are poured into our software development efforts so that we can continue to maintain our technology leading status.

After the team reviewed the model one more time, Caroline summarized it. "Okay, our business model is as follows. We make money by providing online advertising services to our customers on a commission basis. Since our purpose is to lead the evolution of online advertising with relentless innovation, we've built a competitive advantage by focusing heavily on continual innovation. Not only with the newest features we bring to market, but how we innovate internally as well. We provide a large, high-quality ad network and we invest heavily in training to offer our clients a knowledgeable, expert-level service." She looked around the room. "Boy, I can't believe we were missing that last one." She finished with, "We leverage PR as our primary marketing vehicle to spread the word that we're the innovation leader and the clear choice for both now and in the future." Deepak liked it. "I think it provides a clear picture of what we're doing and how we're differentiating ourselves. And although our training has been diluted lately, we're reinvesting resources to shore up that part of the model."

Caroline brought the discussion to a close. "Okay, folks, here's what we're going to do. Obviously we're on to something here. This is just the first pass and I'm sure it'll get better and better as we continue to work on it. Plus, we need to keep monitoring it for market changes. But first let's take a moment to turn our discovery into a real opportunity. Let's let the employees know that we're going to invest in them. Invest heavily. We want UpMarket's people to be the smartest, sharpest, most knowledgeable workforce in our industry. We're going to get our old reputation back—the one we had before all the money clouded our judgment. Let's have a small kick-off party after lunch to announce what we're doing. We've got a new vision, unity and fixed business model. We're going to be unstoppable!"

Primary Focus

Caroline and Nancy were looking forward to dinner on Saturday night, their first time to talk since the whole imbroglio started at UpMarket. Nancy had recently changed jobs and moved back home from Newport while she looked for an apartment in town near Caroline. Tom suggested to Caroline that rather than meeting at Starbucks in the morning, it might be easier to meet at his home. If she came over an hour earlier on Saturday afternoon, they could meet before dinner. Caroline was eager to see their new home, so she readily agreed.

The Hamiltons lived in a wooded part of Weston. Their home was a beautiful blue colonial with a balcony on the second floor sheltering the front entrance. Caroline drove up the long driveway carefully to avoid the contoured, flat rock wall that traced it to the right. The landscaping in the expansive front yard was beautifully designed and meticulous. Although their home was large and stately, it had a warm personality and inviting appeal.

"Come on in! Great to see you! I'm really looking forward to tonight." Nancy's excitement boomeranged back to her.

"Me too. I hear Blue Ginger has had rave reviews in Boston Magazine for years." Nancy invited her in. "Dad's in his office, but let me give you a quick tour first." That's just what Caroline wanted to hear. "Let's do it!" Ten minutes later, they were outside Tom's office. Caroline had fallen in love with the home. It was gorgeous.

Every room was striking, with high ceilings and magnificent hardwood floors and beautifully furnished. Tom's office had floor-to-ceiling windows along two walls that overlooked the acreage in his backyard. The other walls were covered with dark mahogany paneling and a custom-built Georgian bookcase. His dark desk was perfectly polished, set off by a light-brown leather desk chair, tufted and trimmed with brass nails. It looked comfortably broken in, as if it had spent many long hours in contemplation with him. As they walked in, Tom was standing by the half-empty bookshelves and bent over an open box of books.

"Thanks, honey." Tom said to his daughter, putting his book on the desk. "Caroline, how are you! How are things going?" "Great, thank you, Tom. First, I just wanted to say that I love your new home, it's beautiful!" Tom looked around proudly. "Thanks, Caroline, we're just starting to get settled in. Slowly but surely it's feeling like home. So, how's UpMarket doing?" Caroline was excited. "It's going well and I can't wait to tell you!" Nancy jumped in before they got started. "Okay you two. Caroline, I'll see you in about an hour, not a minute more!" Caroline responded with a smile. "Sounds good."

Tom motioned Caroline to two facing chairs. She was talking excitedly before she even sat down. "Tom, we've not only started to see results from the changes that we made, but as it turns out, the team gets more energized every day. The vision is taking hold and the employees are having fun again. And, here's the best part, they're working harder than they have in the past year. Sometimes I walk into an office late at night and have to tell them to go home. And even then they stay just to finish what they're working on!"

Tom was savoring her excitement. "That's great, Caroline. That's exactly the kind of environment that you want to create for your people. So many companies have a difficult time motivating their employees. They feel that the employees should be happy just to have a job. Or they think if they just celebrate some holiday event, then that's enough. Motivating and engaging your employees requires more. And, I know that you have a natural talent when it comes to that. You have a real ability to bring out the passion in people."

Caroline blushed. "I really do enjoy connecting with everyone at my company." Tom nodded. "That's great because passion is at the core of any business. Without passion, without great people, nothing in business exists. In fact, every act, event or occurrence, comes down to people. People run the company, invest in the company, build the products, sell the products, market the products, service the products, and customers buy the products. Most of what a company is stems from people."

Caroline instinctively knew he was right since she felt the same way. "Absolutely, and the more motivated, passionate and committed your employees are, then obviously the better your company will do." Tom complimented her. "Hey, who's teaching who?" Caroline smiled. "In all of my businesses, I always knew that there were many things that you couldn't control like the customers, competitors and suppliers. But you can always control how you treat your employees, even without a lot of money. Who you hire, for what reasons, and how you motivate them. When you spend time investing in your people, you create an environment that motivates them and they'll build fantastic products and provide outstanding service. Invest in your people and everything else flows from there."

"You know Tom, when we first started UpMarket, we were a team, a very tight team, and it felt like we could overcome any obstacle. I know we lost that right after taking the investment, but we're getting it back now." Tom nodded, "Good. Let's build on that momentum and discuss some of the ways to motivate and engage your employees. The first step is to have an inspiring vision. We've already covered that. But there are several other things you can do."

Tom organized his thoughts for a moment. "An important component to a company's culture is defining its core values." Caroline interrupted. "Do you mean ethics?" "Kind of. Core values help to unify everyone in your company. They characterize the collective beliefs and talents of your employees. They reflect the best of what your employees have to offer, what they do naturally, what they take pride in, and they establish a code of conduct and operation. For example, it may be a passion for world class customer service, a focus on innovation, a penchant for constant learning and improvement, or integrity."

Caroline thought for a moment. "One of the things that really binds my team together is a focus on innovation. They always seem to be blazing a trail and leading the industry and solving problems that have never been solved before." Tom added, "Exactly, and I'm sure they do it naturally and it's something you bring out of them. Core values also act as guidelines for a desired behavior. A company should live those values every day and reward those who exemplify them. And when the employees' core values correlate with the vision of the company, that's a powerful combination. For example, the fact that your purpose is to 'lead the evolution of online advertising with relentless innovation' and your vision is…" Tom hesitated and Caroline finished his sentence. "…to provide the software hub at the center of all digital and interactive media." Tom winked a thank you and continued. "…and one of your core values is innovation, they dovetail perfectly." Caroline beamed.

"Core values also provide a context for decision making. The employee's actions are either in line with the company's makeup or they're not. Sometimes you're forced to make tough decisions regarding employees, but if done properly, it reinforces the core values for all the other employees. Whether there are sixty employees or sixty thousand, the values serve as a guide for the company on what is acceptable behavior."

Caroline knew exactly what he was talking about. She had just lived through it. "In our case, one of our other core values is teamwork. John Chen wasn't living up to that value and therefore we had to deal with it. At first, his departure was shocking to the management team and employees, and quite frankly, even to me, but we came together so quickly after that and much stronger than before. Jake has stepped up and been a great leader of the team. So in the end, it made us stronger and bound us more tightly together."

"Exactly Caroline. And teamwork is probably the last competitive advantage available to any company on this planet. And it's probably one of the hardest to achieve. With great teamwork, politics melt away, people aren't afraid of conflict, and they can quickly and professionally say what's on their minds to get to the bottom of issues. The team can overcome obstacles on a daily basis. If you create a strong team, underdogs can beat champions. Compare that with a team suffering from selfish leadership or debilitating politics. Those companies get nowhere."

"Tom, when it comes to my employees, there are some things that I do that are very simple, but have a significant impact." That comment intrigued him. "Like what?" "I remember their names. And I talk to them. I'm interested in how they're doing. And regarding business, I ask them questions, ask for their feedback and if it's a good idea, I implement it. It's the most basic thing, costs nothing, yet showing them that I care makes all the difference. At many companies I know the employees are viewed only as hired hands. And in those instances, the employees reciprocate in kind with the same disinterest in the company. There's no connection. Those companies aren't even tapping a fraction of what their people can contribute."

Caroline and Tom were still deep in conversation when Nancy knocked on the door. "Aren't you guys done yet? I'm hungry." Caroline and Tom looked at each other. They knew they could go on for hours discussing business. Tom looked at Caroline while motioning with a nod of his head towards Nancy. "Go on Caroline, enjoy yourself, try the Butterfish. It's fantastic." Caroline smiled and then looked at Nancy. "Sure thing, I'm hungry too." Before she left Tom's office she turned and faced him. "Tom, I was really enjoying our conversation. Passion truly is at the heart of any company." "That's right, Caroline. And you foster it naturally."

Culture Club

The email read, "How about we take our management team meeting on the road and meet at Pacini's tonight at 7pm for an awesome Italian dinner?" Caroline wanted to treat everyone to dinner because they had been working so hard. It was mid-August, about six weeks since that fateful board meeting that set everything in motion. The email replies came back quickly. "I'm in!" "Count me in." "I'm there!" The six of them loved Pacini's, their favorite Italian restaurant in the North End of Boston. They were all in a good mood looking forward to Marco and Mother Pacini's authentic Italian fare.

After they ordered drinks, Keith started the dinner off on a high note. "I just want to tell everyone that my sales team was fired up at the weekly sales meeting this morning. The new training is starting to make a difference and the release is gaining traction. Nice job Jake." "Thanks Keith, I'll tell the developers, it'll be really motivating for them. As a matter of fact, if I corraled them together for just a few minutes, would you mind telling them yourself? They'd love the attention and hearing it right from you would mean a lot." Keith accepted the invitation. "No problem, glad to do it."

Deepak asked Beth, "How's our customer service coming along? I know we brought on a couple of new customers this week and with the holiday season approaching the call volume must be ramping up." Beth looked up from her Blackberry. She was reading one final email before putting it away for dinner. "Actually, that's just what I was checking. The two new customers are doing fine, but the call volume is definitely getting to us. I wish we could get around the hiring freeze and add some new Call Center reps." Andrea sympathized, "I know it's tough, but we need to hang on for a little longer. If sales keep gaining traction and we can get back on plan sooner than later, then we may be able to start hiring again." Caroline agreed. "That's right, Beth. We can't afford the new hires now, but maybe we can help you dig into the cause of the call volume and see if there's some way to lessen the burden. It may be only holiday related, but there may be some other things we can do to lower the number of calls as well." Beth hesitated. "That's okay, Caroline, let me see what I can figure out."

Marco, the head waiter knew the UpMarket team well and graciously welcomed them back. After highlighting the specials on the menu he began to take their orders. Approaching Deepak first, the marketing director said loudly enough so everyone could hear, "I'll have the veal scaloppini and my marketing budget back, please." Everyone laughed, but Caroline knew that beneath the joke he really meant it. His team had been working with nickels and dimes and they had a lot of ideas that they wanted to bring to life. "Hang in there," Caroline said again. "We're making progress everyday now."

After Marco left, Caroline thought it was a good time to bring up the topic of the "meeting." "Hey everyone, let me get your attention please. We've been doing a lot of things right over the past few weeks and I think we've even started to have a little fun again. People seem motivated and we're building momentum. And something I'm really proud of is that we've brought our culture back to life. As I was thinking about it, I came up with the idea that it might be helpful if we tried to crystallize it on paper. It'll not only help the new employees at UpMarket get a better feel for our roots, it'll help when we start hiring again to get new recruits into the fold sooner."

Deepak thought it was a great idea. "How do we get started?" Caroline led the way. "Let's go around the table, one at a time, and suggest an adjective that you think describes our culture." Andrea volunteered first. "Integrity." Beth seconded it. "Yes, I like that, great way to start Andrea." Keith went next. "Knowledgeable." Caroline agreed. "One of the key facets of our company's culture, something that we take great pride in and need to spread amongst the new employees, is being experts in online advertising." It was Jake's turn. "How about 'Driven'?" Andrea liked that one. "Good one Jake." Glances were exchanged around the table. The adjectives were uplifting and they wanted to see if the others were enjoying it as much as they were.

Next was Beth. "Innovative?" Andrea snapped her fingers. "Good one Beth, how could we forget that one? That's something that we do naturally as well." Now all eyes were on Deepak. "Okay, I guess I'm up." He thought for a moment because he wanted a good adjective, but he was trying to find one with a little marketing flair and that made the choice harder. Finally, he knew he was taking too long and blurted one out. "Candor! One of the things that I really like about our team is that we can pretty much say anything to one another as long as it's for the good of the team." Caroline liked how this was going. "Nice one, Deepak!"

The stream of adjectives continued off and on throughout dinner. It was motivating to be talking about the culture that they had collectively created. It was something they owned, something that made them special and they were quite proud of it. Andrea had taken notes and was just about finished rewriting them when dessert came. "Hold on, everyone, hold on. I'm ju...ust about done here. Okay, got it. Here's what we came up with. Let me read it back and see what you think."

"Integrity is most important to us. We speak with candor and clarity. Our people are ambitious, very driven and have loads of energy when needed. We are passionate, knowledgeable, and are incredibly tenacious. We simply do not give up and are unwilling to fail.

We embrace change and adapt easily, we embrace learning and we're good problem solvers. We're creative, vibrant, genuine and intense. All of these qualities are what make us so innovative!

Our culture is inspiring and empowering and we welcome people that take responsibility. When we're not so serious (which is a lot of the time!), we use humor to lighten the load. Our people are client-focused, trustworthy and respectful of others. We take pride in our work and we're team players. We're personable and our clients like that. It also helps us work with each other and keep synchronized since we're often in constant motion."

There was silence after she read the compilation. After a brief moment, Keith commented. "Wow, I like that. I can sell that. That's the kind of company that customers buy from." Everyone knew he was kidding—Keith thought he could sell anything—but on a deeper level he sincerely meant it. Everyone was bound by this common culture they had created together. And they were proud of it.

Latitude

"Reed, this is Caroline, how was your vacation?" Caroline was calling from her apartment. He was back from South America and it had been two weeks since she talked to him last. "Good, good, I almost broke my back falling off a horse, but that's a different story. How are you doing? How's UpMarket doing?" Caroline had caught him in a good mood. "We're doing okay. Everyone is banding together and working hard. Our revenues aren't quite where we'd like them, but they're climbing. Jake nailed the first software release and is already working on the next one. He's doing a fantastic job. By the way, I'd like to make him our permanent CTO. What are your thoughts on that?" Reed responded, "Well, the proof is in the releases. If he's getting the job done, you can't ask for anymore than that. If you're sure he's ready for it this time, you might as well make it official." Caroline was happy for Jake. She wanted to reward him for the great job he had done and for his loyalty over the years. He deserved it. And she was also pleased that her own instincts had proven right.

Reed wanted a better update on the most telling metric. "Now, let's get back to those revenues. You say you're making progress, but how far back are we this month? Do you think we'll have a chance at making one of our monthly targets any time this year?" Caroline knew the question was serious, but the way he said it jokingly made all the difference. He would never have been so lighthearted with her two months ago. Caroline took the ribbing well and gave him the revenue details. She felt a thread of a connection with Reed starting to reappear. And, he didn't mention anything about the new CEO. Was that good? Or was there something in the works that she'd soon find out about?

Innovation At Work

"About a month ago, Sam in our Call Center group approached me with a pretty creative idea." Beth opened the discussion at their monthly Innovation Meeting. "When he started here, he went through our humble training program and after taking calls for a few weeks, he realized something. You know our software gives the customers basic information such as ad click-through tallies, response rates and total campaign charges. That's all good, but what they *really* want is the information behind the campaign. Like what's tucked away deep inside our internal customer service systems."

Caroline knew these meetings were vital to UpMarket retaining its innovative edge. She started them a year ago as a way to get employees' ideas, those affecting the entire company, into action. During the course of each month, ideas bubble up to the VP's to get presented at this meeting. The merits of each idea are heard, and after a good deal of debate, the most promising projects are selected and prioritized for testing, and if successful, implementation. Beth continued describing Sam's idea.

"For example, they not only want to know what day the ad ran, but what time of day. And not only what time a particular ad was clicked on, but a graph of the click volume throughout the day. And not just which websites ran the ads, but on what pages of the websites. And so on. Sam saw the pattern and realized that a lot of customers used this information to fine tune their campaigns. And he wondered why we have a person as a gate between our customers and the information they want. Why not develop it so they can get it themselves? That way, anytime day or night, our customers can have immediate access. It'll be more efficient for both them and us. We've analyzed the calls and found that we could reduce our call volume by 21%! This idea reduces our costs, enhances our service, and most importantly, gives our customers more of what they want…greater insight into their campaigns!"

Caroline was proud of Sam. "You know, the very first time I approached him in the Call Center he hinted he was working on something. It sounds great, but have we asked our customers what they think? And, do we have any idea how long it'll take to develop?"

Deepak inserted himself into the conversation. "Beth ran this by Keith and me a few weeks ago. We've had our teams survey the customers and overwhelmingly they said they'd love it." Caroline could see that they were on to something. "Jake, what're your thoughts?" "Well, it's not complicated stuff. The problem is that we're a little jammed at the moment. It's more of a scheduling issue than anything, but we can slip it into the queue." Caroline took the lead. "It doesn't seem like there's much debate on this one. Should we make it official and select this as an innovation project?" Everyone nodded in agreement. "Okay then. Sam's initiative, 'Customer Transparency Release 1.0,' just made it on the list for action." Caroline thought to herself, if only there were more time, more resources, the number of innovations they could bring to market was limitless.

Blind-Sided

September was considered by many to be the best time of year in New England. Mornings are cooler, but the days can be as warm as summer. The slowly dropping temperatures magically morph the green leaves into vibrant reds, yellows and oranges. It's a time of change. Tom and Caroline met on Saturday at Tom's home office once again. They had been working together a little more than three months now. While they continued to make progress, the battles were intensifying.

"Tom, it seems like I can't catch a break this week and everything is starting to come to a head. First, all eyes are on revenues. I need to get them growing more quickly. The forecasts we made at the beginning of the year projected revenues to increase every month. So even though we're doing better, our targets are through the roof and climbing. It would be one thing if I had all the time in the world, but I'm down to $1.3 million in cash and I need to get the company to break even—now. It's like watching sand fall through an hourglass and I'm running out of time.

If revenues don't climb soon, we'll need a layoff to reduce the burn. I'd hate to have to do that to any of my employees. They've all been so loyal and don't deserve it and a layoff would be so demotivating to the ones we keep. And, of course, our competitors would have a field day with that. They'd make sure that every one of our customers found out and that could trigger a death spiral. And, I've got a board meeting coming up. Obviously as the cash balance gets lower and lower they're getting more and more nervous. My relationship with Reed is starting to improve, but it's still very tentative and I'd say it's a pretty safe bet that he won't let cash go below $1 million with me at the helm."

Tom agreed. "It does seem like you're making progress, but we both know that we have to preserve the cash." Caroline persisted. "Wait, there's more. It's Marlin. They just raised $20 million out of the blue. They barely have 10% of the customers we have, but they raised it because of the GM deal and they're being aggressive as hell. They've already enticed one of my software developers away from me and they're going after others. Others on my sales team!"

Tom began, "Caroli…," when she cut him off again. "Actually, there's more. Our arch-nemesis, Xenic Systems, seems to be putting all their time, money and energy into building out their ad network. They're tired of losing business to us and they've had it. I've heard through the grapevine that they're going on a crazy, win-at-all-costs drive to match the size of our network in a copycat move. If they do that, we'll lose one of our differentiators. There," she sat back finally, "that's what's been on my mind."

Tom digested it all, thought for a moment, and said rhetorically, "Hmmm, not easy fighting multiple battles at once, is it." Caroline nodded. It felt good to unload that on someone, especially Tom, but she was doubtful that even he could help her deal with this. Just as she was starting to make progress, she was running out of money, *and* her competitors were raising boatloads of cash and coming after her.

Relentless Persistence

Tom wasn't fazed. "Okay, so there's a lot going on. Let's not get flustered. We need a plan to keep growing revenues while defending ourselves against Marlin, Miami and Xenic. While we're at it, let's see if we can put a little pressure back on them." Caroline pulled herself up on the edge of her chair. "What are you thinking?" Tom pondered for a moment. "What we need is a strategy that leverages all of our strengths and stakes out the high-ground. Who's been helping you with your strategy up to this point?" Caroline, embarrassed, paused before answering. "Well, to be honest, it's not that formalized…it's done mostly on an as needed basis. If someone on my team gets a good idea, we'll either meet together on it right away or schedule some time to discuss it at our next management meeting. Or sometimes we just don't get to it…" Tom tried to keep from wincing visibly. "I guess the good news is that you're not alone. A lot of companies don't meet formally or regularly to discuss strategy. But that's no excuse. You're going to start now."

Caroline took the free pass. "Great. I have a couple of thoughts. For example, we've been talking about lowering prices to take away clients, specifically Marlin's, before they get any more traction." Tom wasn't enamored with price-cutting. "Sometimes that approach works, but often it can be short-sighted and end up hurting more than helping. That usually only works when you have a low-cost advantage, like exclusive access to materials or talent. And, if Marlin has a fresh $20 million in the bank, your strategy wouldn't affect them for quite a while and you might be out of business by then." Caroline straightened her back and came to attention. "Out of business?" She had been dealing with the possibility of losing her job, that was stressful enough, but she never imagined that UpMarket would ever go out of business!

Tom didn't react to her comment. "Besides I want to talk more about a general approach to strategy for a minute, not a specific tactic. We need to think it through, just like we did with your business model. We need to review the key aspects of a good strategy and determine what we think is going to best propel the company forward. And we need to document it to formalize it. That way everyone in your company can read it, learn it, contribute to it, and make it happen. And obviously, we need to develop this strategy with the existing people and resources that you have available. We're going to keep this very straightforward."

Caroline interrupted, "Tom, since we're starting at the beginning, I might as well ask you the first question of all. I know what strategy is, but I'd really like to hear your take on what a good strategy is." Tom smiled. "Good question. People definitely have different interpretations of terms like these. Let's make sure that we're on the same page."

Tom sat back in his chair and thought about his answer. It was a basic question, but he wanted to do it justice for Caroline. "As we've talked about, a business model defines how your company makes money. It defines the value you provide to your customers and how you deliver that value. But strategy takes that one step further. It conveys how you're going to protect and improve your business model. It's a roadmap showing how you plan to drive your company towards its vision. And it details how you plan to allocate the people and resources at your company to accomplish that."

Caroline spoke up. "My business model is how my company operates today. How I make money. My vision is where I ultimately want to be. And my strategy is the bridge between the two or my plan to get there." Tom confirmed it. "That's right. Now, shall we get started on that plan?" Caroline pulled out her pen. "Let's do it."

Tom stood up and paced as he talked. "First, let's set a few guidelines. I'm going to walk you through the process of developing your strategy, but once we're done, you're going to want to get this in front of your management team and work on it. You need time to let it sink in, get additional feedback, and validate some of the assumptions we're going to be making, okay?" Caroline gave him a quick nod. "Okay then...our strategy is going to define the borders of the company. Some company strategies plan for expansion within existing markets, others plan to engage new markets, and some do both. For us, since we're a small company in a big, growing market, I suggest we focus on gaining a competitive advantage right here...even if it is a little challenging. The basic question is, how do we make sure that the customers continue to prefer our products and services? What's our innovative idea? Or is it a lot of little innovative ideas? How do we enhance the business model to increase the value we provide and differentiate ourselves in front of the customers? Especially in light of what Marlin, Miami and Xenic are doing. How do we make it an easy choice for customers to select us over them?"

As Tom talked, he was searching in the drawers of his desk. Eventually he found what he was looking for. Tom handed Caroline another two page template. "Just like the business model template, I created this strategy template. It'll give us an outline to structure our strategy."

Strategic Plan

(Devise the plan to match capabilities,
resources and talents in the company)

Financial Objectives. Growth vs. Productivity

_____
_____

Financial Targets:

Revenue Growth: Gross Margins:

Operating Margins: Positive Cash Flow:

Capex: EPS:

Market. Define playing field. What's the overall health of the economy? Will changing govt regulations impact us? Grow existing products in current market? New products in existing market? Engage new markets? Where is each market on the growth curve? What's our position in the market (leader, follower, unknown)? Have we gained or lost market share?

_____
_____
_____
_____

Customer. What are the drivers for increasing or decreasing demand? Will customer segmentation create deeper relationships, more growth? Are there new features we should develop or new technologies we should bring to market?

_____
_____
_____

Products, Services. How do we further differentiate? What are customers seeking in a product/service? How do we expect their needs to evolve? Are there any substitutes entering the market? Should we sell, merge, acquire, partner?

_____
_____
_____

Competitors. What are their strengths and weaknesses? How well are they doing and why? What changes in features, technologies or people have they made over the past year? What changes are they likely to make in the future? With whom might they sell, merge, acquire or partner?

_____
_____
_____
_____

Revenue Model. Can we build complimentary revenue streams?

_____
_____

Strategic Plan

(Devise the plan to match capabilities,
resources and talents in the company)

Raw Goods. Do we have a cost advantage from suppliers? Do we have an access advantage from suppliers?

_____
_____
_____
_____

People. Do we have the right people for where we want to take the company? Should we make any new hires? How does our talent compare with the competition? What are we doing for training? What are our incentive plans?

_____
_____
_____
_____

Processes. How do our costs compare to the competition? How do we lower costs? Increase quality? Increase speed? Gain capacity?

_____
_____
_____
_____

Distribution. Is it wider? Faster? Eliminated? Partners?

_____
_____
_____
_____

Expense Model. How do we allocate our resources to create a competitive advantage?

_____
_____
_____
_____

Caroline knew the drill and she led the conversation from there. "Financial Objectives. Well, we know that growth is our primary objective, but we only have so much money in the bank, so we can't do it at all costs like Marlin. So we also need to focus on productivity and on doing more with less." Tom interrupted. "Caroline, you know your business model really well now. I suggest you sit down with your team to jettison anything that's not directly related to your business model or this pending strategy. Make sense?" Caroline agreed. "Perfect sense. And when it comes to these financial targets, I'll spend some time with Andrea to find out where we stand now."

Caroline paused and thought for a moment. "Tom, I just realized something, we can't even attempt to project future targets until we finish developing our strategy, right?" Tom was glad she caught that point. "Exactly, Caroline. Only then will you know, what your real investment is, and in what areas, as well as where you expect to cut costs and how. At that point, you'll be able to make projections on the expected returns. And if the projections aren't what you expected, and you feel you need to be more realistic or more aggressive, then you'll need another iteration, or multiple iterations until they come in where you want." Caroline flipped over the first page to look at the rest of the template. "You know, Tom, we did a lot of this research when we reviewed our business model." Tom was waiting for that. "That's what makes it so straightforward. Now all you have to do is think 'protect and improve.'"

Caroline's eyes lit up. "Protect and improve, huh? I've got something right in line with that. Actually, it's probably our biggest innovation yet. Behavioral Targeting. Jake and his team, along with Deepak and his group, have really outdone themselves this time. It's where we monitor the activities of the website users and what pages they're visiting to get a better understanding of their likes, dislikes and interests. You know, their behavior. That way we can help our clients target their customers with ads that are more relevant to them. I've been speaking with Jake and I think we have a real game-changer here. You see, there are some competitors offering Behavioral Targeting, but the volume of traffic we carry and the way our systems are architected, gives us a huge insight advantage on the users' behavior."

Tom probed deeper. "Sounds like it could be big, but before we get too excited, have you and your team spoken to the customers, is this something they want?" Caroline's smile grew wider. "Absolutely. I spent a great deal of time on the road the last few weeks and took the opportunity to ask each of them for their feedback. It was the same response from everyone—the sooner the better. Advertisers want it because it increases the likelihood of a website visitor clicking on their ad and thus generating a better return for the campaign. And, the more formal confirmation is that Deepak and Keith have been surveying and interviewing the clients getting the same feedback as well."

"Jake feels that the way our systems and ad network are structured, our solution is highly unique and not something easily recreated by our competitors." Tom knew she was on to something. "Caroline, how long do you think it'll take Jake to build?" Caroline had a cunning smile on her face. "That's the best part. Jake has been working on this in his spare time for the better part of six months. He has a prototype that works and he's already shown it to his team. They think they can develop the beta version of a commercial product within thirty days! Even just the advance notice that we're coming out with this will help sway clients in our direction."

Tom reveled in the thought with Caroline, thinking of how the innovation might propel them technically even further ahead of Marlin, Miami and Xenic. "Sounds like a no-brainer. And there's a side benefit. Even if Xenic does catch up with the size of your ad network, by the time they do you'll have implemented this and leapfrogged them once again!"

Caroline was in command. "You're right, but I have a separate strategy specifically for that. I want to make sure that my team keeps signing up new, high-quality websites to ensure that we maintain our lead on the network side, but there's another angle on this. Xenic signs up any website irrespective of the reputation of the publisher. We've always heavily promoted the fact that we have the largest and highest quality network, but we never quantified high quality! Until now. I'm going to work with Deepak so that we push like mad the fact that we screen the entry of new publishers with very stringent standards. We have a 10-point Quality Assurance test a publisher must pass to be included in the ad network. That way, even if Xenic reached our network size, they'd have to explain-away the fact that their network is mostly Mom & Pop publishers and not very strong." Tom was impressed. "Caroline, that's good stuff. It's very straight-forward and it's largely a matter of positioning, but if you do it right, Xenic will spend most of their time defending the low quality of their network and won't even be able to take full credit for its size."

Tom began testing Caroline. "Now let's take a look at your internal processes. How's your customer service coming?" Caroline was on top of that. "Our training programs are really working well. We're doing things like pairing our experts with our newer employees and everyone's benefiting. Even the experts are learning by seeing the systems through "fresh" eyes. And, we know first-hand that regardless of any competitors' specific advantages in technology or bank balances, it's always a differentiator to be able to speak knowledgably with the clients and solve their problems. It's clearly one of our strategies and it's working." Tom signaled a thumbs up. "Perfect. Full speed ahead there."

As Tom scanned the template and saw the People component, he remembered something Caroline had said earlier in the conversation. "Caroline, there's one comment you made that troubled me and I think we should deal with it now. It was when you said Marlin had hired away one of your employees and was going after others. Overall, it sounds like your employees are pretty motivated and engaged, but it sure would be nice to try to lock them in as much as possible."

Caroline knew where he was going. "I've wanted to attack that for a while now, and I'm going to bring it up with Reed and Mark before the next board meeting. I want to increase the level of stock options for each of our employees and institute an employee profit sharing program, even though we don't have any profits yet. Our employees can see that sales are growing and our burn rate is declining. They can understand that if we all pull together and make it happen, both their stock options and profit sharing could really be worth something. And, I think if we make it attractive enough, it might stop an exodus to Marlin before it even starts. I know through the grapevine that the Marlin products aren't very good and the politics over there are brutal. So, despite their lure of higher salaries, I truly believe that our people will be smart enough to see that we have a better future, and not jump ship, only to be in a worse position a year from now." Tom agreed. "That's just what you should do. If your employees see UpMarket making progress, enjoy their work, and have a stake in a successful outcome, then they'll stay."

It was getting late and Tom summarized their conversation so far. "Here's where we stand. You're going to condense all that we've covered and fill out the Strategic Plan template. In each section you're going to document the specific strategy and next to it, the operational action items, who's responsible for what and by when." Caroline nodded. "Next work on this with your team and get them involved. They'll bring it to a higher level, but remember to always keep it simple. When it comes to strategy less is more."

Caroline had some final words. "You know, Tom, it seems to me that strategy is about making basic choices about how your company competes. Obviously you can't be all things to all people since you only have so many resources, but if you can find some position where you're the absolute best and play to your strength, then you can take market share." Tom said, "Exactly."

Walking into Tom's office Caroline was slightly overwhelmed, but walking out she felt much better, she knew exactly how to compete. The real question was...could her management team pull it off?

Running Straight Into Reality

Caroline spent another few days churning through the strategy. Defensive moves…offensive moves…this idea costs too much…that one isn't worth the effort. For hours, she thought about where the market was going and how UpMarket could be opportunistic. She thought about the capabilities of her company, what resources were available, and what initiatives would be realistic and within their means to accomplish. She went over it until she couldn't go over it anymore. Finally, she called a meeting.

Deepak, Jake, Beth and Caroline were all congregated in the conference room. It was Wednesday afternoon, the soonest that Caroline could get everyone together in the office at the same time. Keith and Andrea marched in a few minutes late apologizing for a late-running billing meeting. Caroline hid her irritability; she hoped to make a lot of progress outlining their strategy so they could start getting it into action. The world kept moving, no time to waste.

She started by reviewing what she had crafted on paper. The team talked about the online advertising market, where it was headed, how it was likely to evolve. They discussed in detail each of the competitors, their business models, where they excelled and where they were lacking and what their next moves might likely be. They talked about their customers, existing and future, what they wanted, what they valued most. They talked about developing the strategy to protect and improve the business model and provide a plan to further their efforts towards their vision. It was a crucial test for everyone and they had to get it right. It wouldn't be too melodramatic to say that their company was under siege. Marlin, Miami and Xenic were coming after them. And for Caroline competing meant more than just keeping her job, or protecting millions of dollars in investment. It meant survival. They weren't going out of business tomorrow, but if they didn't take the right steps today, they could fall behind, seriously behind, and not be able to compete tomorrow.

"Okay everyone, now that we're all on the same page with our strategy, what I'd like to do is have us play devil's advocate and try to catch the flaws in it." She wanted to make sure it could withstand the collective scrutiny of her team. "Make sense?" Everyone nodded. Caroline called out, "Who wants to start?"

Uncharacteristically, Beth spoke up first. "I think there's one thing we should all agree on right from the beginning. We're going to share this with every employee in our company, but many are new to our company and this industry. Heck, many are young and even new to business! So, we should strip out all the jargon and make this plan live on its own without needing a strategy class to decipher it."

Caroline, a little surprised at both the insight and intensity from Beth, was equally enthused. "Great point, Beth, that's exactly what we'll do." Yet, after thinking about it, it made sense to Caroline. Beth liked to develop people. She did it naturally. She could instinctively assess where people were intellectually and what the next step should be for their development. She was right; a complex strategy document wouldn't work.

Beth's comment triggered a thought from Keith. "Caroline, knowing that we're going to show this to all our employees, and knowing what a tight-knit industry this is, what if it leaks out to our competitors?" Everyone hesitated for a minute. Good point. That would surely kill the idea. Andrea took it a step further. "I can see it now. Reed and Mark learn that we gave the plan to our employees and then hear that one of our competitors has our complete playbook. That'll create some fireworks."

Caroline refused to be deterred. "You know, I've thought about that...a lot. And there's two points for us to consider. The first is, if we don't show the strategy to our employees, then we'll be the only six people in the company that know it and there'll be fifty-four others operating in the dark. Imagine the power if all sixty of us knew and understood the plan, were able to give input on how to make it better, and could ensure that we brought it to life? Now that's powerful.

"Secondly, if our competitors know our strategy, then presumably they can take steps to copy it or thwart it. But Dell's competitors have known Michael Dell's direct-to-consumer business model and strategy for decades, yet no one has ever been able to fully recreate what he's perfected or stop his growth from startup to a $40 billion company. And everyone knows that Wal-Mart's strategy is to compete on cost achieved from scale, distribution logistics and inventory turns. Yet no one has been able to fully reconstruct or thwart what they've accomplished either. Copying someone' isn't easy—you not only have to know the strategy, but you have to have the talent, resources, systems, skill and desire to execute it. Frankly, I don't see any alternative but to share it."

Deepak was convinced. "You know it's risky, but I think the potential reward is worth it. But if we're going to do it, then let's not go half way. Let's communicate it, train them on it, and fully engage them. They're the ones on the front lines that know a lot about our customers, products and competitors. If we do it right, they'll make it happen." Having started this line of discussion, Beth ended it. "It's agreed then. We're going to keep it simple and use our strategy to focus everyone in the company on the plans we're making to march towards our vision."

It was a little after six o'clock and the team had been at it for four hours. Everyone was famished. Deepak was the first to break. "Anyone hungry?" Nearly everyone, including Caroline, chimed in. "Yes!" Andrea took charge. "I'll have someone in finance run down to Abe's pizza. That way we can keep going and try to get this done?" Keith voted. "Pepperoni for me!"

The team pressed on through the evening. It was almost midnight and the room was littered with pizza boxes, soda cans, and dozens of scrawled-on pages. Adrenaline had left them. Caroline knew it was time to wrap up for the night so she had Andrea print off six copies of the plan. Andrea passed them out. "Here you go everybody. Note that at the top I inserted our preliminary numbers in the Financial Target section. They're based off of this year's YTD performance as well as the objectives in this plan. I'll run a detailed financial model separately that we'll need to review. Once we have both documents we can make sure they tie together or adjust as necessary."

UpMarket Strategic Plan

<u>Financial Objectives</u>. Growth vs. Productivity

Growth is our primary focus, but not at all costs. Maintain breakeven to 5% operating margins and reinvest any additional profits into growth.

<u>Financial Targets</u>:

Revenue Growth:	*Year 2007: 81%: $10.5m to $19m*	Gross Margins:	*74%*
Operating Margins:	*0-5%*	Positive Cash Flow:	*$310,000*
Capex:	*$375,000*	EPS:	*$0.03*

<u>Market</u>. Define playing field. What's the overall health of the economy? Will changing govt regulations impact us? Grow existing products in current market? New products in existing market? Engage new markets? Where is each market on the growth curve? What's our position in the market (leader, follower, unknown)? Have we gained or lost market share?

Economy expected to be stable. Govt. regulations not a factor. Our focus is on rapid growth within the existing online advertising markets. In 2006, banner advertising is a $16b market growing 35%+ annually and rich media advertising is a $640m market growing 120% annually. Both markets are emerging and encountering the growth stage. We are not the market leader in terms of revenues or market value, but we are positioned as the innovation and technology leader. Our focus is purely in this market.

<u>Customer</u>. What are the drivers for increasing or decreasing demand? Will customer segmentation create deeper relationships, more growth? Are there new features we should develop or new technologies we should bring to market?

The driver for increasing demand is the greater accountability over advertising dollars that online advertising offers. New features to tap that demand as well as increase response rates are: 1) Behavioral Targeting Releases 1.0 & 2.0; and 2) Customer Transparency Release 1.0.

<u>Products, Services</u>. How do we further differentiate? What are customers seeking in a product/service? How do we expect their needs to evolve? Are there any substitutes entering the market? Should we sell, merge, acquire, partner?

Behavioral Targeting Release 1.0.   Accountability: Jake Porter   Date: 12/1/06
Customer Transparency Release 1.0. Accountability: Jake Porter   Date: 2/1/07
Behavioral Targeting Release 2.0.   Accountability: Jake Porter   Date: 5/1/07

<u>Competitors</u>. What are their strengths and weaknesses? How well are they doing and why? What changes in features, technologies or people have they made over the past year? What changes are they likely to make in the future? With whom might they sell, merge, acquire or partner?

Marlin: To beat them, focus on product and service quality and go after GM.
Miami: To beat them, have Marketing tout the full-service story and position them as a niche player.
Xenia: To beat them, maintain largest network lead, but heavily market our network quality advantage. All three will be challenged by our planned software releases.

<u>Revenue Model</u>. Can we build complimentary revenue streams?

For the year, focus on existing revenue streams and efficiently handling growth.

UpMarketStrategic Plan

Raw Goods. Do we have a cost advantage from suppliers? Do we have an access advantage from suppliers?

Not Applicable

People. Do we have the right people for where we want to take the company? Should we make any new hires? How does our talent compare with the competition? What are we doing for training? What are our incentive plans?

Invest in employees, incentivize desired behavior, institute employee profit sharing (defend against Marlin).
Accountability: Andrea Johnson Target: Program Operational Date: 11/30/06

Processes. How do our costs compare to the competition? How do we lower costs? Increase quality? Increase speed? Gain capacity?

Need-for-Speed development initiative to combat Xenics lower cost with speed and centralization.
Accountability: Jake Porter Target: New Process Defined & Implemented Date: 12/31/07

Invest heavily in employee innovation training, on-the-job training, new skills training.
Accountability: Beth Jarvis Target: 4% of revenue Date: 12/31/06

Distribution. Is it wider? Faster? Eliminated? Partners?

Continue to grow network, but focus Marketing heavily on the quality of our publisher websites to position Xenic as having an inferior network (even if they did match our size). Aggressively promote our 10-point Quality Assurance program.
Accountability: Beth Jarvis Target: 3,500 websites Date: 12/31/06
Accountability: Beth Jarvis Target: 6,000 websites Date: 12/31/07

Expense Model. How do we allocate our resources to create a competitive advantage?

Continue to leverage PR heavily as a credible way to position ourselves as market leader, while reinvesting a portion of our advertising dollars into our software development efforts to maintain our innovation and technology leading status.

Caroline took a look at the plan in near final form. "Guys, you've done a great job. I thought what we started with was good, but this is great. This plan really defines our market, where we think it's going and how we want to compete." Deepak added, "Right, and it indirectly shows how we're positioning the company going forward. I'll be able to adjust our marketing plans to fold in perfectly with this."

As a software developer, Jake's inclination was to think things through to the end before embarking on a project. "This is great, *and* motivating, but I know this market changes constantly because our competitors never stand still and our customer's needs are always evolving. Doesn't this plan run the risk of getting outdated?"

Caroline didn't hesitate. "Good question Jake, and the answer is 'yes.' Our plan not only runs the risk of getting outdated, it will get outdated. Now that might be in one month and it might be in twelve months. That's why we need to review it regularly and adjust as needed." Andrea made a suggestion. "Why don't we review our strategy at the same time we review our quarterly financials?" Caroline decreed, "Good idea, that's just what we'll do."

Finally, Caroline ended the meeting. "Let me see if I can briefly summarize the main points of our strategy. Our vision is to provide the software hub, at the center of all digital and interactive media, coordinating the majority of advertisements worldwide. Working towards that objective we're going to focus heavily on growth, but not at all costs, so we want to achieve and maintain a 0-5% operating margin. Our key strength is that we're natural innovators and we're going to focus on continuing to lead the industry. Specifically, and in the near term, we want to be known as the ones that brought advanced Behavioral Targeting to the industry. And we leverage PR heavily as a credible way to position ourselves as the market leader. And we're going to focus on Need-For-Speed development to generate a relentless barrage of innovative releases. We want to maintain our status as having the largest ad network, but we're enhancing our message to make sure we market it as the highest quality network as well. Lastly, we're going to continue to invest heavily in our employees by fully funding a program of continual learning and offering profit sharing." Everyone was nodding. It seemed sound. It was within their capabilities. It seemed like it could work.

"Let's go home. Let's let this sink in for a day or two. I want to make sure that the plan isn't too aggressive and at the same time is challenging enough so that we can make as much progress as possible. And, we need to make sure that all of the operational items attached to each strategy are the right ones and achievable. We'll probably have one more go at this before we show it to the board and then the employees. Thanks and now get some sleep."

Caroline and the team were pleased with what they had accomplished. They developed a great plan, worked hard and even enjoyed it. They had come so far so fast. But there was one last element they were missing. The one that brings everything to life. And they didn't have it yet.

Enough Already!

The first week of October was the earliest that Reed and Mark could coordinate their schedules for an UpMarket board meeting. Caroline kept them abreast of recent progress, but they were eager to look "under the hood" and find out exactly what was going on. Board meetings provided the opportunity for a thorough review of the operations and had an inevitable way of exposing gory details. It was the first week of October and that meant that early financial results for September would be available. Reed sat at one end of the table, Mark at the other end, and Caroline in the middle.

Caroline prompted, "Shall we start?" Mark didn't answer. He had his head down, flipping through the board packet that she put together for the meeting. VCs had a way of doing that. They saw so many presentations in a year that, good or bad, they just had to flip through the deck and jump to the end. Reed answered for both of them. "We're good, Caroline, let's do it."

"Our revenues for September were $849,000 on a revenue target of $1.05 million for a shortfall of 19%." Mark's head was still buried in the packet, but she felt his grimace. She kept going. "We've been holding our expenses reasonably steady for the past three months and they came in at $970,000. This month, we made no equipment purchases, so we burned another $138,000 and our cash balance is $1.322 million."

Mark had heard enough and cut Caroline off. Ignoring her he glared instead at Reed. "Reed, how much longer are we going to let this go on? At our last board meeting we were down to $1.9 million in cash. Now just three months later we're down another $600,000 with the balance at $1.3m! This is crazy! Jeff Stricter at SunWave Software just sold his company last month and he's already looking for his next gig. I say we give him a call and get him in here."

Caroline was shocked, upset and genuinely infuriated. How could he say something like that right in front of her? But she couldn't deny that they were down to just $1.3 million in cash. She had burned through more than $4.7 million over the past year and a half, but they were making progress and about to turn the corner. And she deserved some credit for that. She wasn't going to sit here and take this abuse. She was going to give Mark a piece of her mind.

Reed didn't leave much of a silence. Before Caroline could utter a word, he barged in. "Mark, that's totally inappropriate. If we were to have that conversation at all, there's a much more professional way to have it. Now I think you should quiet down for a while and let Caroline continue rather than just cutting her off after two minutes into a presentation." Mark was fuming. Fuming for several reasons. He was furious that Reed had humiliated him, and worse, had spoken to him that way in front of Caroline. That made him the maddest. Plus, he thought he was purely correct in his reasoning. She wasn't performing. CEO's get removed when they don't perform. Sorry. That's just what happens. Let's do it and get on with it. We have a company to build here.

Reed took control of the meeting. "Caroline, I see this a little differently. Weren't June revenues just a little over $600,000 back at our July board meeting?" Caroline nodded. She was still in shock at what just happened, but she appreciated Reed's support. "So as far as I can see, that means that your revenues are up 40% from the beginning of the summer." Caroline's tense brow loosened. "That's right Reed. That was going to be my next comment before I was interrupted." He continued. "And, I see that you've held expenses reasonably steady and your burn has been cut from $300,000 a month to about $150,000 this month." Caroline was gaining hope and said, "$138,000."

Reed looked up at Mark. "Mark, I'd like to hear a little more about what's going on here at UpMarket. Seems to me like we might have hit a low point at the July board meeting and Caroline has started to turn this thing around." Mark's fury had abated to simple anger, he sat there like a child at dinner who didn't want to eat his vegetables. Reed looked back to Caroline. "When do you think you can get to breakeven and stop the burn without affecting the growth in revenues?" Without hesitation Caroline said firmly, "November. If we keep doing what we're doing, then November should be the month where we breakeven with revenues over a million per month and our low cash balance about $1.1 million." Reed nodded slowly in approval, leaned forward and squinted as if he was trying to get inside her head. "What's your plan?"

It was Caroline's turn to control the meeting again. "First, I want to be up front with you that the holiday season plays a role here. November and December are our biggest months of the year so we'll have some uplift in revenues just due to seasonality. But as you can see from our 40% gain since June, that also means we have some new initiatives that are gaining traction. We fixed a problem in our business model and it's now performing as it should. And we're keeping an eye on it. Our people are energized and we have a new strategy that I'd like to show you. Now I don't want to make any of this sound easy. I need help, a lot of help, from both of you." She knew Mark was smarting from the encounter with Reed and she felt great satisfaction in that, probably more than she should. But there wasn't any reason why she couldn't show him some empathy and try to get him on her side. "I've got one competitor with twenty times the cash we have and another one that's in an all-out war to marginalize us. But despite that, my team and I think we have a good plan."

Caroline passed her strategic plan to both of them. It was very simple, very straight forward, it was realistic and it made sense. They were both impressed, even Mark, who grudgingly offered, "Not bad." They talked about pros and cons and both had some good suggestions. They were particularly enthusiastic about the employee profit sharing plan. Reed promised Caroline the number of the CFO at one of his other portfolio companies where a similar profit sharing plan had been implemented successfully.

At the end, Reed summarized his thoughts. "Listen, Caroline, I'm quite impressed with the turnaround here. I think you're making very good progress and you're on to something. But let's be clear with each other. I'm backing you here, but you have to back me. You have to make this work. Our cash balance is getting very, very low and we're out of wiggle room. If we slide back to the level we were at earlier in the year, then we could be out of business. We'd have to raise more capital and get so diluted that it'd significantly impact our current equity position. Or we'd have to establish some convertible note, but that too would take time, and honestly, by then we would be bringing in a new CEO into a very difficult situation. So here's the deal. I like you, I think you've really turned this around, but you HAVE to make this happen. I'm banking on you. Understand?"

Challenging words, but Caroline beamed inside. The future of UpMarket—and her fate as CEO—was now within her control. Would it be easy? No. She was scared to death. But she was energized and had her confidence back. "I understand perfectly, Reed. And thank you. It won't be easy, but I won't let you down."

Turning to Mark, she said, "And thanks to you, too. I've got to say, I didn't appreciate many of your remarks over the past several months, but whether it was your intention or not, you really kicked me in the butt and got me moving. I won't let either of you down." Mark felt better. He now somehow felt responsible for the turnaround.

After Reed and Mark had left, Caroline sat alone for a minute staring out the window. She was glowing and felt as if she could glide through a 26-mile marathon. During the past summer, she never knew if each day would be her last. Now she was captain of the ship again. Everything was riding on her. She knew she was working hard before, but they hadn't seen anything yet. She was going to make this all work. She couldn't let the employees down, the management team down, the customers, Tom, or herself. Now most of all, she couldn't let Reed down.

Sine Qua Non

It was ten o'clock inside the Weston Starbucks on a bright Saturday morning in late-November. Customers were chatty from the cold and in a good mood with the entire weekend ahead. Caroline sat down while Tom went to get their lattes. While she waited she looked around and was surprised to see the white snowflake decorations drawn in soap on the windows. She couldn't believe Thanksgiving was two weeks away and the holidays were almost upon them. And it had been over four months since she began working with Tom. Every day at work she and her team pushed harder and harder. They were making progress and revenues were growing each month, but she knew they weren't safely through the woods yet.

Tom returned with the lattes and took his seat. As he handed Caroline her coffee he noticed she was preoccupied. "Caroline, what's up?" She nodded to thank him for the coffee and didn't answer right away, still thinking. "I can't quite figure it out. Revenues are climbing, but this industry is growing so fast that we've calculated that we're only growing at the same rate as our weakest competitors. That means we're actually losing market share to those growing faster. We knew that Marlin, Miami and Xenic were coming out with new initiatives and spending, but we've blunted some of them. And I know our products and customer base are the strongest in the industry. Don't get me wrong, there are a lot of things going right and we're in a much better place than back in July, but we should be doing better."

Tom was curious. "Let me ask you this, how do you determine if you're doing 'better' or not?" Caroline didn't need to think about the answer. "It's the monthly revenue numbers. At the end of the month we either hit them or we don't. Either we get closer to our targets each month or we fall behind. It's that simple." Tom made a note and then continued. "Who knows what your operational targets are?" That was another easy question. "Well, we used to have them as part of the financial packet that we review monthly with the management team, but recently we've been spreading the word to the entire company like we did with our strategy." After another note. "Okay, that's good, now if you miss a target, who do you seek out to find out what went wrong?" Caroline was thinking through the process. "Well the management team gets together and we talk about what we think caused the shortfall. We have pretty good insight when it comes to things like that." Tom didn't acknowledge her answer, an infinitesimal hint that she wasn't passing the test. Now she felt defensive.

"Just a few more questions. After you assign a task to someone, when do you check in with them to see how they're doing?" Caroline felt she had a good answer for this question, one that reflected her strong organizational skills. "I enter the task completion date in Outlook and then I get a calendar reminder on the due date to make sure it got done." Tom kept questioning. "One last thing, how frequently do you review your people and what do you assess them on?" Caroline had no idea how that question fit in with the others. "We don't have an official review process, but we do give annual salary increases and it's based on their performance throughout the year." Tom followed on. "But how do you know how well they performed?" Caroline didn't have a great answer and was getting tired of the questions. "You just know, the manager knows."

"Caroline, I'm pretty sure that I know what's missing here. Where you need to improve is with execution. You're simply not executing like you should." Now it was more than her tone that was defensive. "Tom, I've got people working all hours of the night. That can't possibly be the case. These people are motivated and couldn't be working any harder."

Tom let her settle down for a moment and lowered his own voice. "Caroline, that's great, it's really hard to develop motivated and engaged employees and you do that naturally. But your problem doesn't have anything to do with how hard your people are working. It's about how they execute, what they accomplish with all that hard work." Caroline was stymied. "How do you know we're not executing well?" Tom countered. "You just told me." Caroline still hadn't put it together yet. "I told you?" "Yes. My questions were to get a feel for how you execute. Honestly, my impression is that it's the root of your problem. You see, you can have the best vision, business model, a great strategy and very passionate people, but if they don't know how to execute, then it's all for naught. All that effort is wasted." Caroline reluctantly swallowed the fact that Tom felt her company didn't know how to execute and now she was getting slightly aggressive. "So what do you suggest?"

Tom started listing off the tasks like a military general. "First of all, there's communication. You told me that you started to "spread the word," but take it to the next level. It's the people outside of your management team that are doing most of the work. They should know the goals just as well as the management team. So you need to communicate each and every one of your monthly, quarterly and annual goals to every employee. Make sure that EVERYONE, even your receptionist, knows the goals of the company. Talking about goals and performance with employees, asking for input and answering questions, creates an environment where the employees can make better decisions with a full understanding of the consequences. And, they can contribute proactively."

Caroline was no longer angry. She was starting to feel that she had missed it. Tom was convinced he was right. So much so he was talking without taking a breath and she wasn't about to step in front of that. "You can't wait until the end of the month to realize that you didn't hit your targets. Once you find out that you're behind, it's too late. You need to set weekly milestones for every goal and track your progress daily."

"And, just as you talk about transparency in your products for the industry and internal processes, you need transparency into the progress made towards every goal. Then your employees can see every day if they are on track to meet their goals at the end of the month. That's giving them the transparency, the information, the tools to make adjustments before it's too late."

For you, your job is to force constant achievement. When you do that, one day builds on another. One week builds on another. And then all of a sudden, you've made your month. And then the next month. At some point you'll have created momentum. That's the hardest thing to do in any company. Once you build momentum, you're on your way."

Tom wouldn't let go when it came to execution. He knew it was the key to making all the hard work planning, strategizing, motivating and unifying come to life. Making plans and initiatives a reality. "Make sure you follow up relentlessly. Periodically check in with people on their projects. Never wait until the due date to have them tell you that they couldn't get it done. Once again, there's no room to maneuver, no room to adjust, you're just stuck with a missed target. You can't let that happen!"

"And let's talk about annual reviews. It's a must! At my last company I had a sixty-four point review process that every employee went through. One of the review sections evaluated how well they performed when it came to execution. I would rate my people on criteria such as *Faces Reality, Asks the Tough Questions, Sets Clear Goals & Priorities, Sets Milestones, Insists on Accountability, Follows Through, Delivers Commitments, Insists on Quality, Makes Tough Decisions.*" Caroline was taken aback by his intensity and blurted out, "Really, isn't that a lot of work?" Tom nodded. "Absolutely, but you need to establish an execution culture at UpMarket. Reinforce it every day. Execution is incredibly hard work, but it's where everything materializes."

Tom realized he had been talking nonstop. He had trouble turning himself off when it came to business principles he was passionate about. They discussed the details of execution and how to create an execution mindset at UpMarket. Finally, after about an hour, they both got up and walked towards the door. Caroline was still absorbing the conversation. She thought she knew how to execute, but obviously not at the level Tom was talking about. She vowed UpMarket would start executing fully. And immediately.

Conductor—All Aboard!

A broadcast email arrived in the inbox of every employee:

From: Caroline Ford
To: UpMarket Staff
Subject: Company Meeting
Everyone,
Our company meeting will start in fifteen minutes in the
conference room.
See you then!
Caroline Ford
CEO, UpMarket
Our Purpose: "To lead the evolution of online advertising
with relentless innovation."
Our Vision: "To provide the software hub, at the center of
all digital and interactive media, coordinating the majority
of advertisements worldwide."

This was the reminder to the meeting announcement sent out the day before. And a stir again ran through the ranks.

Why was there a company meeting? Would there be bad news, maybe good news? They'd never had the entire company together except for a holiday party or back in the early days when the whole company consisted of just a few people.

The day before, Caroline had taken her management team through the agenda. She wanted everyone, from CEO to receptionist, to be in the full company meeting. Those on the road would be required to dial in. By the end of the meeting, she vowed that everyone would know exactly where the company stood, the operational and financial goals they had set, and the daily, weekly and monthly milestones in between.

"Thank you, everyone, for being on time." Caroline started the meeting at exactly 1pm, signaling to everyone that, beginning right now, all meetings would start on time. It was symbolic of the most basic principles of execution: 'do what you say, when you say you're gonna do it.' If a meeting is supposed to start at a certain time and stragglers file in late, that sloppiness sets the wrong tone for the executional mindset of the company.

"I've called everyone together to communicate our goals for the coming weeks, months and year. We're all in this together so we all need to know what our targets are. And at the end of the meeting, I'm going to announce an additional block of stock options for everyone and a new employee profit sharing program. Without getting into the details right now, simply said, if we hit these goals then everyone will benefit." There were exchanged glances around the room. They were excited about the stock options, but the employee profit sharing was new, uncertain, and people weren't quite sure what to expect. Besides, it was no secret that they were not yet profitable.

Behind Caroline's plan was her knowledge that people craved leadership; that they wanted to be part of something bigger than themselves. She also knew that they wanted more insight into the company and how they could contribute. She reasoned that if people were vested financially, and they could directly benefit from their hard work, then there would be nothing holding them back.

Caroline motioned towards Andrea. "Andrea, please walk everyone through our sales targets, profitability targets and supporting metrics for network growth, development schedules, marketing plans and customer service." "Sure, Caroline. Here we go everyone. These targets have already been posted on our intranet as of this morning and you'll see our progress towards them updated daily. For any goal where we're behind, we'll know exactly where we need to push harder or get more creative to catch up—every day." Andrea took a few minutes to review the goals as well as the underlying drivers of the goals. That way everyone understood the inherent relationships between them, such as how growth in the ad network could impact the revenue targets. As Andrea finished, Caroline was scanning the room. The plan was to get the employees involved. But would anyone ask a question?

Sara, a new member of the ad network team, timidly raised her hand. "Is it alright to give a development suggestion?" Andrea encouraged her, as eager as Caroline to get the conversation going. "That's exactly what we want. Go ahead, Sara."

Sara felt the eyes of the entire company on her. "If our goal is to have another 200 publishers in our ad network by the end of the year, it would be a lot easier to nail that goal if the software that connects them to the network was a little easier to install. If we changed just a few things with it, it would install with a lot less hassle and the customer would be up and running in half the time." Caroline and Beth smiled at each other, realizing they had just tapped the power that comes from getting input from the people closest to the tasks in question. "Great idea," confirmed Caroline. "Jake and Beth, can you arrange a time to meet with Sara to find out what she suggests and how long it'll take?" Both Jake and Beth answered in near unison. "No problem."

Sara raised her hand again as if to keep her place in line.

"And one more thing. There's another benefit to fixing this problem. It'll dramatically reduce the number of customer call backs and stop clogging up the Call Center phone lines." Caroline looked at Beth and Beth knew exactly why. She missed that one. Caroline had wanted the team to help Beth try and figure out the problem. She knew Beth was short-staffed and since they couldn't hire any additional help, the only other alternative was to try and reduce the volume. Caroline vowed to herself at that point—never again—would she fail to dig in where she sniffed a slip in execution.

After a brief moment of silence, a voice came out of the conference room speaker. "Caroline?" piped up Alex from the New York office. "Is that you Alex?" Caroline knew everyone by name and frequently impressed people with her ability to recall facts and details about her employees. Alex was relatively new and the employees were intrigued that in a split second Caroline could recognize and recall exactly who it was over the speaker. "Yes, it's me. I have an idea to generate more sales." Caroline loved to hear that. "Sounds good, what is it?" Alex started in. "One of the things that I'm seeing is that we don't have enough financial publishers in our ad network. Being in New York, we have a lot of financial advertisers and sometimes we don't have enough inventory to fulfill their campaigns. Not only are they let down, because in some cases they lose their budget for any monies not spent, but then UpMarket loses out too. If we focused our ad network team just a tad more on financial publishers, that alone would increase our revenues." Keith was beaming, proud that one of his guys had made such a productive suggestion. Beth looked at Caroline with a firm nod signaling that she would take care of that request. Caroline gave a nod back. "Alex, this is Beth. That's an easy adjustment to make and I'll give the ad network team updated instructions in the morning. Great idea and I'll make sure it happens." Alex was shocked that his idea was accepted instantly. At his last company, they didn't ask for ideas, never mind implement them. "Thanks Beth!"

Next it was Shah who raised his hand. Shah was part of the three-person IT group that reported to Jake. "Yes, Shah?" said Caroline. The young engineer was nervous, but determined to make his point. "Our data center keeps growing to support our customer growth, and some of you might not know this, but we're projected to add another ten servers by the end of the year to prepare for Q1 of next year. My comment is that originally we ordered high-end servers because we thought we needed the horse power, but we've recently found out that that's not necessary all of the time. If we went to the next model down, we could save a couple of thousand of dollars per server." Andrea was all over this one. "Excellent idea, Shah." Speaking to Shah, but looking at everyone in the room she said, "You might have just saved us $20,000!"

Suggestions and comments kept coming. One idea sparked another. Some were great, others not so great, but everyone got into it. Caroline was shocked at the productivity. And there was a huge side benefit to the process that she never expected. The employees were loving it! All they wanted was to be asked for their ideas. To know that if they were good ideas they would be implemented. To know that their ideas contributed to attaining the company's goals. That kind of participation was motivating.

Caroline saved the best for last. "Now for the big news. As I said at the start of the meeting, we're providing additional stock options for everyone and implementing an employee profit sharing program. The latter means that a percentage of our profits will be distributed to you quarterly." She scanned the room to gauge their reaction. "Now some of you know that currently we're not profitable. So there's nothing to distribute at the moment. But we've made considerable progress over the past few months. Now we need to keep pushing and get the company in the black. Once we do that, our destiny is in our own hands. Andrea has prepared an outline that describes how it works and will walk you through it in meetings later this week as well as provide information about the additional stock options. But here's the gist: the better the company does, the better everyone does. Everyone looked around the room. They were a little hesitant at first, but the buzz started to grow. Caroline knew the meeting was a success, but how long would it take to see results? This had to work. Now.

PART 3
ANOTHER REALM

True Grit

It had been about five months since that historic board meeting in July. Momentum was building at UpMarket and despite the daily challenges, there was a general feeling that they were headed in the right direction and making progress. On a Friday morning in early-December Andrea walked into Caroline's office.

"What's wrong?" Caroline asked, alarmed at the look on Andrea's face. "Caroline, I have some serious news." Her heart dropped. After what she had been through during the past five months, bad news could trigger old anxiety in an instant. Caroline anxiously replied, "Get it over with, Andrea, what is it?"

"I just finished the financial statements for November." Andrea said dramatically. "We've shown a small profit!" Waiting for it to sink in, Andrea's expression changed from feigned doom to glee. Caroline didn't like the head-fake, but that was quickly overwhelmed by the good news. She leaped out of her chair and hugged Andrea. "I can't believe it!" Andrea continued. "Wait. It gets better. Even though we're only a week or so into December, nearly all of our executional metrics are above target. At this pace, we'll generate a sizeable profit for the month and start generating positive cash flow next month." Caroline jokingly drove the point home. "Do you mean that we'll actually end a month with more cash than when we started? All from our core business?" Andrea picked up on the joke. "Ya, what a novel idea."

Word Travels Fast

Reed caught Caroline in her office that afternoon. "Caroline, don't go spending it all in one place now." Caroline knew what he was talking about. "News sure travels fast around here!" Reed confessed. "Andrea sent out the preliminary financials today and I saw the small profit. I've gotta tell you, I'm really proud of what you accomplished. You went through a really difficult time and showed some real passion, tenacity and leadership. I'm impressed." Caroline inhaled those words. "Thanks Reed. The entire team pulled together and made it happen. We seem to be operating smoothly right now, and what's more important, we have the systems in place to monitor our performance and adjust as necessary. You know I got a nice call from Mark this afternoon too. He congratulated me on the profit." Reed was a little surprised at Mark's initiative. "Did he now. Well good for him. And good for you. It's a little easier when people aren't slinging arrows at you, isn't it?" Caroline laughed. "You can say that again."

The Fuel of Success

The next morning Caroline walked into Starbucks for her meeting with Tom. For the first time, she had profit news and she couldn't wait to tell him. She had her old smile back once again. As soon as Tom saw her, he knew something good had happened.

Caroline blurted it out. "We showed a profit this month!" Tom smiled and sat back in his chair relishing the news. "Wonderful Caroline. I knew you had it in you." Caroline continued. "And, if we keep the pace that we're on now, we're projected to have a great December too. Plus, we're getting more efficient with equipment purchases and once we start collecting these receivables, we'll be generating positive cash flow. What a relief to know that soon we won't be burning cash anymore. I can think more clearly and my confidence is back!"

"Caroline, positive cash flow is the ultimate barometer of the health of a business. It's the direct result of everything working together: your business model and strategy combined with your ability to execute." Caroline nodded. In the past few months, she had not only learned from Tom, she had lived the lessons as well. "Cash flow is the foundation of your business. Without positive cash flow, you can't hire the people or garner the resources to develop your company. Positive cash flow makes everything possible. It's a direct feedback mechanism on how well you're performing, a kind of "report card" for your company. When you understand how the cash is flowing and from what directions, then you'll really understand how your business is operating and you'll know what changes to make. Generally, unless you're making an investment for future benefit, the stronger your business model, the stronger your cash flow.

Tom grew silent. He realized that this might be his last "official" meeting with Caroline talking about UpMarket. He enjoyed it so much that he was going to miss their discussions. The ups, the downs, the stress, the jubilation. Then he remembered. "Caroline, are you coming to our holiday party this Saturday?" Caroline replied, "I wouldn't miss it for anything."

Benefits of Results

Keith and his wife Jill were slow dancing to the music of DJ Flanagan at UpMarket's annual holiday party. Keith spoke into her ear. "The mood's a little more upbeat than at our Fourth of July party, don't you think?" Jill looked around. "You can say that again." It was Friday night in mid-December and the private room at Pacini's was decorated with white lights and holiday reds, greens and golds. Everyone was in a giddy mood, anticipating a wonderful night. Not only was it the holiday season, and a weekend, but earlier that day they had all received holiday bonus checks. The checks caught everyone by surprise since UpMarket had never handed out holiday bonuses in its short corporate history.

Deepak, handsomely dressed, made a smashing entrance wearing a brand new sport coat, perfectly pressed pants, and a red and green Brooks Brothers tie with a matching handkerchief in his breast pocket. And his "date" for the evening was Andrea. Actually they weren't dating, but lived in the same town and had shared a ride. Andrea, was wearing a stunning evening dress for a change and carefully-applied makeup. The two made quite a pair. Beth and her husband were interrogating the DJ about his playlist. She knew that Customer Service was operating smoothly and she could relax for at least one night without carrying her ball-and-chain Blackberry. All in all, counting spouses, significant others, and last minute dates, there were over a hundred people at the party.

As soon as she saw that the room was full, Caroline took DJ Flanagan's microphone and strolled on to the dance floor. "Everyone, can I get your attention for a minute?" The remaining chatter died down. "Thank you everyone for coming tonight. It's great to see all of you having such a good time. I just wanted to say a few things before you get back to the music and fun." Her voice lowered slightly and her tone grew more serious. "All of you have done an amazing job over the last six months. We started out the year a little shaky, but month by month you adapted and adjusted and did whatever was asked of you. For that I'm so grateful. You're a wonderful group of people to work with and I know we're going to have many great times ahead." She raised the microphone for everyone to give themselves a round of applause.

"Now I have a surprise for you." The room fell silent again as everyone strained to hear. "As you know we handed out holiday bonuses earlier today, but we have another bonus check for each of you tonight." Everyone looked surprised, filled with curiosity. Holding a stack of envelopes, Caroline explained. "These too are bonus checks, although a little smaller than the ones you already received. Quite frankly, I think the average check is in this batch is about ten dollars." A few laughed approvingly. "But do you know what this is? It's your first employee profit sharing check!" The crowd of employees, spouses and friends roared. It wasn't the size of the check, it was the fact that they were profitable for the first time—a sign of victory that they had attained one of their goals together. Caroline scanned the cheering group and smiled with accomplishment. After a minute, she asked for quiet again. "Now our job is to make UpMarket grow, and enjoy that progress every day, and at the same time, make our employee profit sharing checks grow!" Shouts rose from the crowd. "Thanks Caroline!" "Way to go UpMarket." Caroline finished her speech. "Thank you to everyone for working as hard as you do. You can pick up your checks over by the DJ stand. Now it's time to get back to the party and happy holidays!" With that, the music resumed.

It was a special evening for all. The bonuses were the main topic of the excited chatter in the room, but there was joy too. And it was about more than newly found bonuses during the holiday season. It came from a feeling of accomplishment and a sense of being part of something special. A realization that they were among the lucky ones…the ones who actually enjoyed where they worked.

Through The Gauntlet

The next night was the much anticipated holiday party at the Hamiltons. As the cars pulled into the driveway, the festive ornaments and white lighting on the grounds were reminiscent of a picture-perfect holiday postcard. Holiday music played by the Boston Symphony Orchestra floated through the sound system in every room. And in the air, fragrant aromas wafted up from the twelve-foot Christmas pine tree in the living room and the cinnamon-spiced wassail in the dining room.

The house was filled with guests and it took a while for Caroline to work through the crowd and find Nancy chatting with several people she didn't know. After the introductions, Caroline noticed Tom fiddling with an ornament on the tree and politely excused herself from the group. She had a gift for Tom and wanted to give it to him while he was in a rare moment alone.

"Tom, everything looks so beautiful!" Tom gave Caroline a hug. "I'm so glad you could make it, Caroline. And by the way, how's our favorite company doing?" "Really well. Our revenues are climbing, especially during this holiday season, and we're signing up new clients quickly now. We're all looking forward to next year." Tom was pleased. "That's great. And how are Reed and Mark doing?" "They're both good. They're both happy with where we are right now and the fact that they didn't have to go through a major upheaval mid-year. In hindsight, they actually did me a favor. Their ultimatum pressured me into finding you and figuring out things a lot sooner than I would have myself. I learned a lot about running a company. And I learned a lot about the consequences of bringing new investors in to a company. It's both a blessing and a curse and you need to understand their expectations."

Tom saw a different Caroline in front of him than six months ago. This woman had been through the gauntlet and came out the other end much more seasoned. What she lacked in experience she had made up with determination. "That's so right Caroline. A lot of times people raise capital despite not having proven their business model. They'll spend a bunch of money on marketing trying to gloss over the problem and then they find out that their marketing isn't working either. All the while they're burning cash and getting deeper and deeper in a hole. Ironically, it's those startups that have no capital, like UpMarket before the investment, that sometimes have the best chance of survival. They're scrappy and need to find out what resonates with the customers or else go out of business. And they learn how to develop and market their products on little or no budget at all. They figure out what works rather than throwing money at the problem." Caroline agreed. "You said it well. It's a shame that so many have to go through what I went through. And I'm sure that many never make it through, but learn the lesson just the same."

"Tom, I wanted to officially thank you for all that you did for me. I couldn't have made it through without you." Tom winked at her and smiled warmly. "You know Caroline, business is tough…and it gets tougher every day due to the constant change brought on by technology. But when you can grab the hearts and minds of your employees, you can accomplish anything. You've always known that. You've always known that everything in business comes down to *people* and you naturally connect with your employees and know how to motivate and engage them." Caroline took great satisfaction in the compliment and only nodded while Tom went on. "And when running a business, people are counting on you to find the way to win. There needs to be a *context* for them to succeed. They need to know their work has meaning, to rally around common objectives, understand what's important, work with passion, understand how to attain their goals, see progress towards their goals, and have a stake in the outcome. You just needed a little help with the context. That's all."

She held out her hands. "I know that when we started this, you said 'no compensation,' but I wanted to get you something meaningful and thought you might be able to use this." She handed over the neatly wrapped gift box and he opened it. It was a plastic Starbuck's gift card. Caroline quipped, "From now on the latte's on me." Tom smiled. "That's really nice of you Caroline. Every now and then we'll have to meet there and I'll get you a latte and you can tell me how you're doing." She agreed. "Any time."

"Tom, I've got to tell you, I'm going to miss Saturday meetings with my silent partner." Her comment was heartfelt. "Caroline, don't worry, I'll always be your silent partner. Come over anytime you want to run an idea by me. I'd love it." She smiled. "Okay, I'm going to take you up on that. By the way, there's one thing that we never did get to." Tom was curious. "What's that?" "We never did get to that pricing conversation." Tom smiled and even laughed out loud. He looked knowingly at Caroline. She got it. In hindsight, it wasn't about pricing or anything like that. It was about *leadership*.

* * * * * *

Caroline was fortunate to have a Silent Partner like Tom to guide her through difficult times and create a context where innovation could thrive and results could be produced. But not everyone has a willing and affordable mentor at their local Starbucks. What follows is a detailed review of the elements of The System™ and how they can be implemented at your company to create a successful business outcome.

* * * * * *

The System™

While the essence of business is change, change is difficult. When you find something that works, the last thing you want is for change to come along and force you to figure it out all over again. But the message is...get used to it. In fact, create a competitive advantage by embracing it! After all, once you know it's coming, like the changing seasons of the year, it's predictable. And take advantage of the fact that human tendency is to avoid change, overlook an unpleasant reality, and not accept things as they are. Let your competitors be plagued with that tendency, but not you. Companies get into trouble when they run their business model for years on end, irrespective of changes in the marketplace. New technologies surface, a global competitor appears, or substitute products squeeze their way into the market. At some point they can't take the pain any longer and are forced to confront the fact that they've become outdated. Then they need to undergo gut-wrenching, high-risk changes to reengage the market.

The world's economy has changed dramatically over the past few decades and the change is accelerating as technology advancements build rapidly upon one another. From the

1960's through the early 80's, you could learn a trade, land a job, and very often work for the same company for ten, twenty and even thirty years. Defined-benefit pensions were the norm and used as an incentive to maintain long-term employment and to provide a level of personal financial security. Companies competed nationally, management was top-down, and the drivers behind business were achieving scale through standardization and optimization.

Today, workers must continually learn new skills and acquire new knowledge to remain relevant in society. They switch jobs frequently with an average tenure of just a few years, sometimes less. They build their defined-contribution 401ks, organize in teams, take risks, create small businesses and compete on a global level. A new breed of worker is forming that works virtually for multiple companies at once. Maybe it's a software developer, a Call Center representative or a VP of Marketing, but each will leverage their experience and hedge their bets across multiple companies simultaneously. And it'll become commonly accepted by employers as well who desire the same flexibility.

The System™ is comprised of seven age-old, enduring principles of business:

<u>**The System™**</u>

Lead with **Vision**
Streamline with **Unity**
Differentiate with your **Business Model**
Win with **Passion**
Advance with **Strategy**
Harvest with **Execution**
Reinvest with **Cash Flow**

If Vision represents your ideal, Cash Flow represents the progressing manifestation of your ideal into shareholder value. Exactly in the middle, at the heart of the system, is Passion. For passionate employees are at the heart of any successful business. And maintaining that success and ensuring that your company stays relevant lies in your ability to tweak, adjust or completely reinvent your Business Model and Strategy without requiring massive reinvestment, retooling or upheaval in your organization. Staying on top of the change requires constant monitoring for signs of market evolution. The System™ provides you with the context to notice these subtle changes that over time can turn into paradigm shifts. Companies that intentionally create business models to be flexible and opportunity-driven will find themselves able to adapt more easily to the evolving markets and other inevitable challenges.

Together these principles form a system to lead any company, harness innovation, and create a context to manage a successful business outcome for investors, management and employees. They provide a business leader with the necessary tools to guide his or her company to success.

Vision

Every company deserves an inspiring vision. Your purpose describes why your company exists and gives everyone's daily effort meaning. Your vision builds on that and inspires people to reach some greater destination or rally behind a passionate cause. This element of The System™ must be established first as all other elements need to be aligned with Vision to ensure efficiency and focus.

Lead With Vision

Your vision connects everyone in the company and rallies them around a common cause. Since it's a direction you take rather than a goal to be attained or a destination to be reached, it acts as a "North Star" for all employees to know if they are moving in the chosen direction. As a business leader, when you grab the hearts and minds of your employees and show them where you're going, how you're going to get there, and why they should follow, they become motivated to accomplish nearly any task, even if out-manned or under-resourced. And to truly engage, motivate and rally people, your destination or cause must be deemed worthwhile. For if it is, you can inspire people into passionate action.

Building such an environment at your company is straight-forward, but not easy. The vision shouldn't be verbose, confusing, or theoretical. Instead keep it simple, real and exciting. Make sure every employee can easily grasp it, understand it and identify with it. Note that inspirational visions aren't something framed, placed on a wall and forgotten about. They are "owned" by the employees and lived each day. Start by providing the initial, overall vision, but expect to refine it with your employees' help, as Caroline did. The power of unity, buy-in and joint ownership comes from the actual process of discussing and building the vision together. When you do, it becomes a living, breathing rallying cry as well as a tool to unleash the passion in people.

Unfortunately, too few companies have a stated purpose and vision that creates a cause, a mantra, a reason for coming to work enthusiastically each day. A bland vision, or for that matter, the complete lack of a vision, manifests itself in several ways. A lack of unity around corporate objectives is less apparent because there's no single unifier. Employees lack motivation and the concept of "work" to them is merely a place to earn their livelihood. Business models and strategy lack impact and direction and precious resources are squandered on irrelevant objectives.

Living the vision everyday requires consistency. All business decisions should be made in line with and in support of the vision: hiring, firing, project selection, acquisitions—everything. That's why, as important as the other elements are, they can't be properly developed until the vision of the company is in place. That way, all efforts and energies move in unison in the same direction. It provides context for all your decisions to ensure there's minimal waste of valuable time, money and effort.

If your company is in business to fulfill an important, noble or great vision, that's inspirational for all involved. For example, Herbert Hoover's vision of "A chicken in every pot and a car in every garage" in his 1928 presidential campaign was a vivid way to communicate his desire that everyone would be prosperous under his presidency. Establishing a company solely to make money is lacking and doesn't provide a business leader much fodder to lead his or her people through the tough times that ultimately ensue. While the obvious objective of business is to make money and generate shareholder value, that objective can be more easily obtained if it is the result of a greater ambition instead of the sole aim.

Unity

Unity is a term to denote agreement within and among the company's major constituents—shareholders, board members, management and employees—across the key issues that govern the company. While the issues are many and varied, the most notable are vision, expectations for exit valuation and timing, compensation and mergers and acquisitions. For each issue, stylistic and strategic differences abound and can either strengthen the company if coordinated properly or seriously impair it if disagreement runs its course.

Streamline With Unity

<u>Vision</u>. Your board members, management team, and employees all need to be aligned around the company's vision. If your senior executives disagree, then secret mandates can manifest, politics run rampant and resources become divided. If your board members aren't aligned, then competing strategies are offered and differing business models discussed.

<u>Exit Timing & Valuation</u>. Unity is required around shareholder expectations. If your shareholders, board and management fall out of unison on expected exit timing and

valuation, the company can fall victim to inner turmoil, strife and politics. One group could be pushing the company to show short-term performance with greater profitability because its members want an earlier exit. Conversely, another group might want to see reinvestment in the business, less attention to profits, and day-to-day decisions rooted in long-term planning. Strategy, investment and resource can't be focused appropriately until expected exit valuation and timing are agreed upon.

<u>Compensation</u>. A new level of cooperation is required today between employer and employees. In this new paradigm where continued innovation is the antidote to accelerating change, employees need to come to work each day with the same zeal for improvements as their managers. Working purely for salary or hourly wages will not create the level of thinking and participation required. With entrepreneurialism thriving worldwide, people are working in smaller teams, with the big differentiator being that more and more people are working for equity at smaller companies. These people take risks, realize there's no job security, and compete to win for survival. They are incentivized to contribute everything they have to innovation and to making the company more competitive. New initiatives, slogans and mandates aren't strong enough motivators. If employees are simply doing their jobs, collecting their pay, and going home disinterested, then innovation is nowhere to be found.

All employees, regardless of title, need to be incentivized to promote continual improvement. Sales incentives, bonus programs, rewards programs and certificates are all worthwhile, but two things that outshine all of these are stock options and employee profit sharing. These two compensation components reward more than individual performance, they reward team effort and success. They focus all of your employees on the collective progress of the company. The more profit your company generates, the more your employees will be compensated, but conversely when the company faces difficult times, everyone from top to bottom faces difficult times. Management needs to view all employees as in *partnership* with them to create shareholder value.

With stock options and employee profit sharing in place, every action taken by an employee is viewed through a revenue generating or profit-driven frame of mind. Employees naturally become more innovative for their own financial benefit. They even start to hold each other accountable financially. Some question if giving up a percentage of profits to employees is in the best interests of the shareholders. However, it's been proven that motivating and engaging employees, especially toward greater productivity and innovation, will generate greater profits for shareholders. Studies show that companies with highly engaged employees significantly outperform those with lesser levels of engagement in terms of operating income, net income and EPS.

> *ISR conducted a study of 664,000 employees worldwide over a 12-month period. They analyzed the operating income, net income and EPS figures between companies with highly-engaged employees and those companies whose employees had low engagement scores. Companies with highly-engaged employees improved operating income 19.2%, net income 13.2% and EPS 27.8% over the 12-month period. Those with low employee engagement scores showed declines of -32.7%, -3.8% and -11.2% respectively. (Source: www.isrinsight.com—July 2006)*

Motivated employees increase a company's productivity and profitability. They produce higher quality work, stay at companies longer which reduces recruiting and training costs, have better safety and attendance records, and establish stronger customer relationships.

<u>Mergers & Acquisitions</u>. Is it better to acquire or develop from within? M&A is a hotly contested and divisive issue under any circumstances. Some board members are fiercely against mergers and acquisitions. They feel that most acquisitions aren't successful, too expensive, and integrations are too

time-consuming and distracting while the more focused competitors run unencumbered. Instead, these board members like to see revenues grown organically. They feel it's a more efficient way to expand. Others feel that mergers and acquisitions are the fastest way to build a business and create scale. The majority of risks are borne by the smaller companies and once the innovation or model is proven, the larger company can acquire the successful entity. Synergies create shareholder value and the combined concern either strengthens an existing market position or provides more safety through greater diversification. Straddling the two opinions is another point of view that certain mergers and acquisitions make sense at the right time for the right reasons at the right valuation. It's important to know where your board members stand on this issue.

Unity requires teamwork on many levels: among the board, management and employees and teamwork within each of the constituents. Unfortunately, countless companies have been seriously and negatively impacted by a lack of unity around the issues mentioned as well as others. Quickly reaching unity is necessary to advance the company. Obviously, not everyone is going to agree all the time. That's natural and healthy. There may be personality conflicts, ideological conflicts, stylistic differences, or people, as always, just holding on to differing points of view.

However, here are some thoughts to work through substantive disagreement: 1) Communicate frequently since discord often breeds simply from all parties not having all the facts; 2) Confront disagreement early and directly never allowing it to fester. The earlier you detect lack of agreement and do something about it, the better the chances are for a healthy outcome; 3) Look at the disagreement from the other perspective; 4) Seek resolution by finding the areas where you do agree and giving it the majority of your efforts; 5) Think win-win and in terms of abundance rather than scarcity or adversarial competition; 6) Focus on the future by developing an action plan that places the focus on the resolution.

Normal discourse on these subjects is warranted and breeds better results, but out-and-out, long-running disagreement can be dangerous. Tempers can flare around these issues since all shareholder and employee interests are at stake. Unity is certainly not a "touchy-feely" element. If constituents are aligned, your company can move through the competitive landscape like an arrow through the wind with minimal drag. If constituents are not aligned, competition is focused inward, progress slows and the company can even unravel.

Business Model

Defines how the company makes money and characterizes the company's core activities and unique structure. It represents the value a company provides its customers and how that value is delivered to create a sustainable competitive advantage with profits above the industry norm.

Differentiate With Your Business Model

Your business model is the engine of your company. It represents the core activities of your business and describes how your company makes money. It does so by defining the value your company provides to your customers (i.e. revenue) and how that value is delivered to your customers (i.e. expenses) to generate a sustainable competitive advantage. When developing your business model, focus on the core activities where you can tangibly differentiate and excel beyond your competitors. Make sure that those activities matter to your customer, for only those will be the primary drivers of profitability. And, of course, align your business model with your vision. For example, if part of your vision is to be the worldwide cost leader of widgets, then you wouldn't choose to promote high-cost, differentiated products, expensive distribution channels or excessive marketing.

When developing your business model the objective is to create a sustainable competitive advantage by generating profits above the industry norm. Note that more than one company can share a business model, but the implementation of the business model can vary widely with differing results. Closely examine your competitors to learn how they uniquely solve the customers problem, and do so at an appropriate cost level, to generate profitable and sustainable revenue. What resources are present such as intellectual property, employee talent, customers and brand equity? What capabilities are present such as efficiency, quality or customer service? Learn the expense models of those winning in the marketplace. What's their mix? This process highlights how your model compares and what adjustments you may wish to make.

Keep in mind that the premise of the business model is to identify how to profitably provide value to your customers by solving their problems and needs. A sound business model requires a thorough understanding of your customers' needs and how those needs are expected to evolve over time. And accurately predicting the changing needs of your customers over time is what allows you to stay relevant in the marketplace. While it's often an advantage to be slightly ahead of the curve and first to market, it's important that you're not so far ahead that you've invested in the wrong areas and your predictions fail to materialize. Even if you act somewhat cautiously, as long as you can adjust quickly—a sign of strength in any business model—then you can stay relevant and profit in the market.

If your business currently participates in just one market with just one product, then your company is overly exposed to the evolving competitive threats and customer needs. A stronger business model includes multiple revenue streams from a variety of products that appeal to a wider customer base. That way if any one product is compromised due to market, technology, customer or substitute changes, the others provide safety through diversification.

When using your business model to examine market changes, the first objective is to determine if the fluctuations in the market are cyclical or structural. Cyclical changes vacillate with the ups and downs of the economy while structural challenges represent markets in irreversible decline. As you would expect, with technological change accelerating, more and more markets are experiencing structural change. Structural changes require a significant change to your business model. And the further entrenched you may be, the more difficult the change.

A negative trend in your cash flow (unrelated to new investment) is the indicator that something is wrong with your business model. The earlier you can detect the problem, the better, thus strengthening the case for routine review. Your review should attempt to isolate the cause. The market may have evolved, a new competitor surfaced, a substitute product introduced, or a new technology developed. Possibly your cost structure has increased due to increased supplier costs, ramped-up employee wages, higher fulfillment costs or less efficient internal processes. Maybe buyers have aggregated purchasing power or quality and service levels have declined. Ultimately, customers don't perceive the value in your products or services at the same price they once did. Given the constant barrage of new technologies, it's easy to see that a business model is an evolving thing. In just the last 25 years, VHS tapes were replaced by CDs which were replaced by DVDs, which are being replaced by MP3s and so on.

With your business model providing the foundation of your competitive advantage, it stands to reason that it's the place most subject to continual innovation. Either one or more components to your business model can be improved or even the entire business model can be renewed. While some of the best innovations can arise purely accidentally, or from a problem or crisis that needed a solution (every adversity has a way of birthing a possible advantage), many arise from a planned individual effort or a group brainstorm. Since the first two are unscripted and impossible to predict, let's discuss the latter.

When researching how to innovate, look to entrepreneurs. First, the average startup is under-funded and lacks sizeable budgets for R&D, marketing, travel or any expense line item at all. Money flows from hand to mouth and resources are thin. Second, the same startup is often denied access to many of the things that mid- and large-sized companies are accustomed to and take for granted: access to the best, most expensive employee talent in the industry, key suppliers that require large minimum orders, key technologies where existing patents eliminate certain methods of development, or marquee customers that prefer to work with established vendors. Third, smaller companies constantly fight against time. Large companies have staying power from existing capital and positive cash flow that they can use to outlast smaller, struggling concerns, tie them up in court, or renew their customers to long-term contracts.

With all of those obstacles to overcome, it's no wonder that smaller, starving, struggling startups come up with the best innovations! There's no alternative! They lack money, they lack access and they lack time. Established companies think in terms of the resources and advantages that they possess while small startup companies think in terms of how to get around those resources and advantages and break into the market. Breeding innovation requires that everyone in your company think like an entrepreneur with his or her back against the wall. Small companies are unencumbered by process, policy and budget hurdles, not to mention tradition, and don't think in those terms. They think in terms of free-wheeling ideas, a clean whiteboard, and an open mind. Train your own employees, no matter how large your company, to search for innovation throughout your business model with the universal mindset of "no money, no access, no time." And rest assured, right now there's more than one small competitor thinking how to get around your advantages. If you think it can't be done, know that many out there are trying to figure out a way. One of them will.

Passion

The greatest force in business. Almost every aspect of business—ranging from designing, marketing and selling products to servicing customers, managing finances and implementing new business processes—depends upon the people performing the action. How they perform in their jobs is the primary competitive differentiator. Most of the value in a company is made up of intangible assets which include the employees, corporate culture, product brands and customer relationships.

<u>Win With Passion</u>
Think about it. Other than the hard assets on your balance sheet, the majority of your company's assets lie in the hearts and minds of your employees in the form of corporate culture, brands and customer relationships. If the majority of your company's assets result from the actions of your people, then it stands to reason that the more motivated and engaged they are, the stronger your assets and the better performing your business will be. There are many things that you can't control in business, such as the overall economy, direction of a market, or a competitor's advances, but what you can

control is how you select, train, motivate and engage your people. Since most everyone has access to capital and near equal access to information, how you motivate and engage your employees is a true competitive advantage in business.

How is passion defined? It's what drives the underdog to win the competition. It's what allows the under-funded startup to beat the well-capitalized market leader. Passion encompasses conviction, enthusiasm and an energy that is difficult to quantify and compete against. Passion emerges from employees who are committed to your company, believe in the vision, and take pride in their work. Passionate employees love their job and can't wait to get to work in the morning. They overcome obstacles on a daily basis and, whenever necessary, expend the extra effort. They talk positively about your company and spread the word to friends and colleagues. They are excited at the prospect of achieving something great and even more motivated when they know they have a vested outcome in the success of the company.

Conversely, unmotivated and disengaged employees not only are a drag on your company, they can actively impair its progress. In the United States, studies show that nearly three-quarters of all employees are either not engaged or vocally unhappy with their work place. They show up to work each day and do what is expected, but little more.

> *"In the United States, just 29% of employees are energized and committed at work, according to Gallup poll data. Perhaps more distressing, 54% are effectively neutral—they show up and do what is expected, but little more. The remaining employees, almost two out of ten, are disengaged."* (source: www.gallup. com—April 2004)

Workers who are actively disengaged can cause discord and harm. They can't wait for the first break of the day and spend most of their day planning what they're going to do once they leave the office. Productivity slows to a crawl and they can dismantle customer relationships easily. These employees can very negatively impact a company if their discontent spreads.

If the environment within your company doesn't foster motivated employees, it's time to make a change. Unfortunately, it's usually the best employees that leave first. The churn created by employees leaving can significantly erode profitability. Your company loses its investment in recruiting and training, intellectual capital, customer relationships and company knowledge. Losing good employees (and the inherent investment in them) can happen in an instant, and mitigate all of your hard-won savings created by other initiatives.

So why are so many employees just neutral on their company or even actively disengaged? It could be that the average CEO in a major corporation makes several hundred times what the average factory worker makes in the same company. It's not hard to see that employees can develop animosity because they feel that management is only out for themselves. And, the actions of management at Enron, Worldcom and others over the past few years help fan these feelings. But even with these examples, the issue is seemingly more basic and widespread, and in many cases, easier to combat.

Many vendors offer solutions to enhance employee motivation and engagement:

- Human resources and survey firms conduct employee engagement surveys, compare results to statistical norms, perform analytics and provide post-survey action planning.
- Consulting firms help develop performance strategies, provide leadership coaching for senior executives, teach employees to identify and develop strengths, create performance evaluation systems, develop succession planning, and design compensation systems.
- Award sites offer rewards programs to enhance

employee loyalty including holiday gift programs, loyalty rewards, thank you and instant recognition programs, rewards credit cards, service recognition and achievement rewards, plaques, certificates and gift catalogues.

- Life coaches train people how to function in a difficult workplace through such goals as striking a life/work balance, staying fit, creating a pleasing work environment, and making new friends.

These are all meaningful initiatives, but real impact can be made when the company creates a context for its employees to succeed and engages them fully. With The System™ in place, everyone knows where the company is headed, how it's going to get there, what values guide the way, and if the plan is on track.

Employees need to adjust to the new paradigm as well. They need to accept that the world is changing every day and that they must keep learning and growing to evolve with the company or be left behind. It's better for employees to be proactive and help the company with its innovation efforts rather than be handed a two-week termination notice from a behind-the-times company undergoing enormous structural change. Innovation leads to growth and growth means more opportunity. Fortunately, most employees recognize this modern-day phenomenon and are eager to be part of it. Old jobs can be retooled into new jobs. Of course, positions may be eliminated, but with proper innovation, twice as many new positions may appear.

The key to innovation and a successful company lies in the happiness and motivation of your employees. Continually invest in and develop them. Even beyond the fact that it's motivating for them, if you build great people then they'll build great products and provide outstanding service. What matters is getting results by building loyal teams that can "get any hill." If a business leader can get all employees rowing the boat in the same direction, with passion and tenacity, the company can accomplish nearly any goal and always beat the competition.

Strategy

Provides the plan to protect and improve your Business Model and march the company towards the Vision. It needs to be simple, straightforward and play to the company's strengths.

<u>Advance With Strategy</u>

If created properly, your plan should protect and improve your Business Model and advance your company towards its Vision. There should be Unity and Passion around the plan, it should be able to be Executed with your company's existing talent and resources, and it should generate the desired Cash Flow.

The basis of the strategy is determining which markets you will engage and establishing the borders of the business. Within these borders you can then determine how to allocate your resources so that you effectively compete and differentiate yourself to win your customer's preference.

Keep your strategy simple and straightforward. A bad strategy executed well is a waste of time and resources. A good strategy executed poorly isn't any more effective. When it comes to strategy, less is more. If the strategy is too complex, if it requires a three-ring binder to present, it'll be more difficult to communicate, comprehend and execute. Even administratively, it'll take too much time to develop, review and maintain. Conversely, there's elegance in simplicity. The trick is to have a simple strategy that you believe will work and then execute well.

Play to your strengths. Protect and improve your business model in customer segments where you have the greatest amount of expertise and resources. Great strategy doesn't require that you be a mastermind. It simply means focusing on what works and avoiding what doesn't work. While it's prudent to allocate some resource to mitigate your weaknesses, spend most of it on projecting your strengths.

As a business leader, it's your job to identify the "high ground" in the marketplace and take it. For example, a technology advantage. Be sure that the high ground is worth winning, but when you recognize opportunity, seize it. Take decisive steps with a sufficient amount of resource.

Create buy-in with your strategic plan by developing it with the people closest to the customers and tasked with implementation. They best understand how your customers' needs are evolving and know the intricacies of the execution. This process not only creates a sense of ownership, it garners valuable input while judging if the plan is realistic and within the capabilities of your company.

Innovative companies develop cultures that embrace change. And they take their cultures seriously enough to make them part of their strategic plan to perpetuate the advantage. The hallmarks of an innovative company, are constant learning, speed, and experimentation.

Incorporate a theme and set of initiatives around constant learning and personal growth in your strategic plan. Constant learning pays dividends in many ways. First, studies have been done that show an investment in training enhances a company's bottom line. Second, customer service levels improve because your employees are more knowledgable.

Third, constant learning allows your employees to thrive in dynamic work environments continually churning out new products. Fourth, it makes them want to give back to the company because they realize that the company is making an investment in them.

Out-and-out speed is different from haste. Haste denotes sloppiness and causes more work. Speed creates opportunity because you're able to change on a dime. Speed is critical in terms of external activities such as good procurement, product fulfillment, and customer service as well as internal activities such as reporting, product development and operations. Speed also offers advantages that can overcome a competitor's size and access to resources. Speed allows you to build new technologies quickly, get to market first, land the customer, and be responsive with customer service.

Encourage informal innovations to run freely and without structure. A suggestion to change policies or practices may need appropriate approval, but the concept is to allow them to flower as unencumbered as possible. For larger innovations, those affecting more customers or more components of your business model, innovations need a more formalized process. Establish a funnel-like system to channel innovation, a system for accumulating ideas, selecting the best, testing and then implementing the winners.

With this process, routine experimentation becomes part of your daily operations. Google runs a similar model. At any one time, the search engine giant has hundreds of projects brewing with small teams entrepreneurially pushing them along. They're tested in the real world with a fraction of the daily search volume. Out of the hundreds of projects, those spiking with a return are isolated and more fully funded for further development and implementation. Via this process, innovation is built into the core of the company which allows it to evolve at a rapid rate and stay accurately tuned to customer demand. The concept is to avoid making huge bets on new technologies; instead, make many small bets and see how they pay off. Initiatives that hit the vein then earn greater investment. It's a way to keep innovation at your core and allow you to constantly evolve, but not make high risk bets that imperil your company.

Once you've completed your strategic plan, review it to make sure that there's a balance between short and long term goals and that it's realistic. A common mistake business leaders make is to embark on an aggressive plan where the ambitions don't match the company's resources and capabilities.

The essence of any strategy is trying to foresee the future of your market and likely customer needs, and then make the necessary investments to position the company to benefit. To do so, consider the technological advancements in your industry and where they might come from. Attempt to determine if supplier costs will increase, your distribution channel will remain viable, expected quality will change, or capacity will grow. Examine the ramifications of a possible acquisition and then consider all the possible M&A combinations your competitors might make. All of the above provides insight into possible offensive or defensive moves. And above all, seek out ways to differentiate your business and increase your margins.

Execution

Execution is the power zone of your company. It brings the other enduring elements to life and can generate unlimited capability. Expertise in execution gives you confidence that you can effectively implement changes to your Business Model and Strategy. Execution is a coordinated set of practices, a mindset, and a part of your company's culture.

Harvest With Execution

Execution is like game day. You can practice all you want, but on game day you must perform. Being good at execution simply means you're good at getting things done. Conversely, companies that don't execute well fall apart: people can't rely on one other, become frustrated and lose confidence in the company. Failure to meet promises ruins credibility and demoralizes everyone. Below are a few rules to achieve tight execution:

Establish an Execution Mindset. The mindset of a company that executes well is one of disciplined pragmatism, hard work, creativity and relentless determination. People at this kind of company confront reality by viewing the world as it is and not as they would like it to be. They avoid politics and are able to ask each other difficult questions that surface issues before they manifest into problems. They are able to make difficult decisions, especially when they involve individual conflicts, to ensure that the greater good is served. They take pride in living up to their promises.

<u>Focus for Effectiveness</u>. Focus brings efficiency. There's no time, effort or resource wasted on things that do not contribute to your quest of attaining your vision. Focus brings results and achievement because sufficient resources are able to be devoted to the prioritized tasks at hand. The opposite is true when a business leader disperses the available resources across too many tasks. When overreaching the capabilities of the company, while the intentions may be viewed as aggressive, driving, and ambitious, there's a setup for eventual failure.

<u>Set Clear, Realistic Goals</u>. When stated goals are unrealistic, employees know it immediately and the project is off to a precarious start. What's more unfortunate is the false optimism of the leader who believes that the employees can pull off the impossible. When it becomes obvious that the goals cannot be accomplished, reality sets in. At that point, it's too late to adjust in time, and credibility is lost. When establishing timelines, begin with the goal and work backwards to the starting point. If in doubt as to what might be a reasonable goal, start with small steps and build from there. Most importantly, involve all the people responsible for the goal when creating the plan. You'll court trouble if those who have to execute the plan don't have a say in its development.

<u>Move the Right People Into the Right Positions</u>. It's a key to execution. The right people overcome obstacles day-in and day-out. They are creative, hard-working, and motivated by achievement. They have a can-do attitude with the ability to adjust on the fly. These people don't need to be managed or shown what to do every step of the way. Simply set the goal with them, ensure their thinking is robust, be available for

guidance, and let them go. Those who can execute tackle initiatives head-on. They are smart people who understand where the company is going, provide valuable advice and get the job done. Select those individuals who know how to block out all the noise and focus on what's important. Select those who are able to gather the right people and resources to get the job done. These people derive great satisfaction from being productive and achieving. The right people know how to execute and it's very motivating and unifying. Others want to be on their team because they show results and win.

Use Milestones, Metrics & Transparency. Milestone provide a roadmap, with checkpoints, for employees to know if they are on track to accomplish their goal. Ensure that each of the milestones is linked to one another logically and builds upon one another. The shorter the milestones (within reason), the more quickly a problem will be uncovered. Using milestones is the same concept as dividing and conquering. It allows you to show progress throughout the project and keep the team motivated.

Charting your performance demonstrates continual progress. Keeping measurements transparent is highly motivating and instills even greater confidence for the team to keep pushing. If a company is not performing at the necessary pace, the employees need to know as soon as possible. Transparency alerts them to trouble at the earliest possible moment and enables them to adjust. If the problem can be overcome, the whole process instills confidence. Whenever they next encounter difficulty, they expect to overcome it again and succeed. A committed team, empowered to act and then resolve a problem, is a group of employees with a sense of control over their destiny.

Knowing that you get what you measure, ensure that the metrics you track are the ones most in line with what you're attempting to achieve for your shareholders. For example, market share growth may be a good metric, but if the company is operating in a commoditized market and each gain in market share actually costs the company money, then it is not a complete or positive metric.

<u>Push   Constant   Achievement   and   Communication</u>. Employees want to know what's going on and how their company is performing. If you can communicate tangible progress, even small, it's motivating to the employees to see themselves a step closer to the overall goal. Employees love to see positive movement and it motivates them to push even harder. It lets them know that the strategy is working and your company is winning. As the progress accelerates, momentum is developed. When employees sense momentum, it spurs them on to even greater achievement. Establishing and maintaining momentum is one of the hardest, yet most critical things, for a company to achieve. Showing continual progress, even if small, is what instills confidence and a can-do attitude.

<u>Accountability</u>. A company always struggles to find its way if people are not held accountable. If no one is accountable, there's no way to determine why the results weren't achieved. If more than one person is accountable, then non-productive finger pointing ensues. For every task, no matter how large, there needs to be a single person deemed responsible.

<u>Follow Through</u>. In reality, there are times when things go undone, even at companies with a stellar reputation for execution. It may be due to a lack of communication, an absence of established priorities or a simple mistake. The objective is to reduce these missteps to an absolute minimum. Follow through rigorously and build into your culture an environment where the team can rely on one another to deliver on promises.

<u>Overcome Obstacles</u>. A key to execution is single-minded determination. If you want results, you must overcome any and all obstacles with tenacity and not allow them to become excuses for failing to meet your objectives. In the end, either you get results or you don't. Expect obstacles when it comes to execution. If there weren't any, then everyone would be able to execute with the same facility. It takes two things to

work through a daily dose of problems. The first is a set of passionate employees, who provide the energy and desire to overcome the problems. The second is the ability to see through to the heart of the matter.

Align Rewards with Performance. What gets rewarded gets done. If your employees have stock options and profit sharing opportunities, their objectives are inline with the shareholders which are increasing profitability, increasing cash flow and increasing equity value.

Create An Execution Culture. Even if you have hardworking and bright people, they can be ineffective if the company doesn't place a premium on getting things done. Create a culture where people aren't afraid to give all the facts and confront each other with the unvarnished truth. Void your conference rooms of politics and encourage everyone to speak in a direct and straightforward way. Ensure that your annual review process rates people on their ability to execute. Create an environment where your best, brightest and hardest workers thrive. Demand that people know their stuff!

Share financial information so that employees have the benefit of information to make decisions. Public or private, large or small, companies all benefit from sharing as much information as possible. Whether it's at the company, division or group level, employees need this transparency to know how their actions are impacting the results. Some executives are uncomfortable doing this, but it's difficult to harness the power of employees if they are operating in the dark. It's not just sharing the financials for sharing's sake. By doing so the employees know that they are trusted and empowered to improve the company. It removes the curtain and shows the employees that everyone is working together towards the same objectives.

In many organizations key information is only made available for the executive team to develop, review and monitor. But let's face it: management doesn't always have all the answers. By receiving input from her employees, Caroline garnered a greater variety of viewpoints. Everyone became obligated to understand exactly how their job impacts the bottom line and that it's not just management's responsibility to generate profits, but the responsibility of all. A company of owners was created.

How do you know when you're not executing?
- Financial targets go unmet
- Deadlines slip
- People stop delivering on their promises
- Cash flow is negatively impacted
- People avoid responsibility
- Blame game is rampant
- Decision-making abilities decline

In the end, execution is about discipline and facing reality. The hard facts are not always easy to come by, and just as importantly, when you do get the facts, they're not always easy to accept. Sometimes we get lax or afraid, and tell people what we believe they want to hear. Or we keep hoping that the situation might improve. In either case, that may avoid the immediate confrontation, but the situation often worsens. It's better to face the unvarnished truth and deal with it head on. Proper execution is about establishing the proper expectations upfront, exposing reality every step of the way, and then executing with a military-like discipline.

Cash Flow

Reflects the aggregation of all the enduring elements of The System™ and how they fuse together to generate a return for shareholders. It's the ultimate barometer for the health of your business.

<u>Reinvest With Cash Flow</u>

Cash flow is the ultimate report card on the health of your business. It's a cold, hard way to monitor performance.

When large investors seek great companies to invest in, they search for those that generate a real return on investment. They seek companies that have a dominant position in an industry, a strong balance sheet, sustainable earnings growth and strong cash flow. Real shareholder value can be produced at a company with these characteristics. Strong cash flow is the tip-off that the other attributes are present.

Cash flow is a no-holds-barred metric of your performance. Earnings can be "manipulated" by how and what you depreciate or amortize, how well the company handles tax planning, how much deferred revenue is in the pipeline and so on. But cash is cash. Cash is king. Either you have it or you don't. Either it's flowing in your direction or you're burning it monthly.

Is there such a thing as too much of a good thing? Can too much cash flow be considered a negative? Sometimes. There needs to be agreement between the shareholders, board and management on the appropriate levels of cash flow. If cash flow is too strong, it may mean that the company is harvesting an unusual market opportunity without reinvesting properly for the next opportunity.

For example, Microsoft had created such a juggernaut that it accumulated $40 billion in cash generating almost $1 billion of cash per month. Although an astounding feat, shareholders didn't want that cash in the bank, but rather, to be reinvested to generate above market shareholder returns. This means reinvesting the cash in strategic acquisitions or making significant investments in new technologies. For five years Microsoft's stock price languished despite having monumental sums of cash. Ultimately Microsoft returned the capital to shareholders in the largest dividend recorded in corporate history. But at the same time, Google became a major threat, probably the biggest threat since Microsoft's inception. Was Microsoft too slow to reinvest or would it have occurred anyway? Nobody knows, but it does trigger the discussion of striking the right balance between appropriate levels of cash flow and new investment.

If growth is your objective, then it's imperative that your company keep reinvesting a percentage of your cash flow back into innovation. That's what keeps your company growing, evolving, and adapting to the changing market landscape. Once you stop the reinvestment, it signals the end of your desire to compete in the marketplace and the new objective of harvesting cash to return to the shareholders.

Summary

The principles of The System™ take time to develop and implement within a company. Very often in the process, all involved would prefer to be dealing with the more immediate issues of their day-to-day jobs. But they shouldn't be pushed aside. With these principles in place, employees can be motivated and engaged. They'll know their work has meaning (Vision), rally around common objectives (Unity), understand what's important (Business Model), work with passion (Passion), understand how to attain their goals (Strategy), see progress towards those goals (Execution), and have a stake in the outcome (Cash Flow). These principles are about leadership by engaging the hearts and minds of your employees. And, more than just "feel good" principles, they can help business leaders guide their companies to success through the challenges created by our intensely competitive global economy.

A Note On Raising Capital

Raising capital to fund and build businesses is part of capitalism and a building block of entrepreneurialism. Unfortunately, rather than using capital to propel forward the small businesses that have established traction, it's sometimes used as a means in and of itself. Businesses without sufficient customers, an established business model, and experienced management are frequently funded and ultimately struggle despite the capital. A great waste is suffered by the investors and it places enormous pressure on the business leaders.

If capital is beneficial, but only at the right time, then when is the right time? What determines when a company is ready? In some cases, an experienced business leader receives early funding, either pre-revenue or before the business model is validated, and can be trusted to create a first-mover advantage. For others, a company is ready only after the business model has been validated and is generating profits and positive cash flow. In those instances, capital is used to accelerate, not create, the initial success.

A lack of capital is not always a bad thing for new companies. Surviving everyday requires that you have a thorough understanding of your business model. And learning to market products on a slim budget forces you to be creative, pinpoint the exact audience, and hone the precise message that resonates with them. Once again, when the successful formula is found, an influx in capital will boost the already positive results.

For companies receiving venture funds before the business model is established and marketing has created a return, too much cash in the bank can create a false sense of security. Initiatives are established, offices opened and people hired... just because they can be. A large capital infusion has a way of masking the true dynamics of a business. Flaws in the business model are not always caught and exposed early on as the capital reserve buys time. Money is wasted on ineffective marketing as the capital induces sloppiness.

The experience of a company becoming funded with new capital parallels the experience of an individual winning the lottery. The new money purely accentuates existing habits, good or bad. After a few years, there are countless lottery winners who find themselves back where they began and even in greater debt. They focus on purchasing items rather than making investments. Their mindset, habits and current state before winning the lottery was simply magnified. Yet there are others who win the lottery and are able to use the proceeds to build a greater, stronger financial position, give to charity, and pass on the winnings for generations.

The same holds true for companies. If the company is missing any of the seven principles of The System™, the new capital isn't used as efficiently as it could, which places unnecessary pressure on the company and investors. If the company has a compelling vision, a unified set of constituents, a sound business model that generates cash, a strategy to grow and a culture of execution to bring it to life, then capital can provide fuel, lock up market positions and generate significant shareholder value. It's the competition between angel and venture capital investors to lock in promising companies that incentivizes them to get in too early. That's why it's a part of their model that several of their investments will be failures and a few will show stellar results to generate the aggregate returns.

When raising capital, it's imperative that you find investors who align with your vision, goals and desires as well as those of the other current shareholders. The objective is to establish Unity right from the beginning or avoid the investment all together. You should have a definite understanding of how much capital you need to raise to meet your business plan objectives and not raise less, which may jeopardize execution, nor more which merely increases dilution. Thoroughly "vet" the prospective investors on criteria such as compatibility with your vision, growth objectives, and management style. For example, explore their commitment to a philosophy of treating employees well and compensating them appropriately with stock options and profit sharing. And the investors should be willing to provide the necessary time, expertise and effort to assist the company by providing valuable input on strategy and implementation decisions. In the end, as long as the valuation options are within reason, the right partners are more important than the right valuation among investor candidates.

About The Author

John Roland is a serial entrepreneur and has built and sold both heavily venture-funded businesses and boot-strapped, organically-grown businesses. Most recently he was the President of FastChannel Network, Inc. A venture-backed, software company, John drove a highly-innovative culture to grow the company from startup to $25 million with 200 employees—an annual growth rate of 110% in a declining market. As the innovation and technology leader, FastChannel merged with DG Systems to solidify its position as the leading provider of advertising distribution services. The merger was approved by the SEC in May 2006 and is a public concern (NASDAQ: DGIT).

Prior to FastChannel, John was the President of Genesis Business Systems, Inc. Genesis, a software company, was boot-strapped from the startup phase and sold to Achieve Healthcare Systems in 1996 to form the leading provider of long-term care automation systems. John has been published in trade magazines and his works have been read by business leaders in over 40 countries.

John lives in the Boston area with his wife, Connie, and their three children, Cole, Kendall and Taylor. To learn more about John and Insight Marketplace, please visit <u>www.insightmarketplace.com</u>. If you'd like to contact John directly, he can be reached at <u>john@insightmarketplace.com</u> and truly welcomes your feedback.

Made in the USA